MW01699410

WONDERWORLD C

INDIAN VEGETARIAN CUISINE

JYOTI NIKUNJ PAREKH

NAVNEET

NAVNEET PUBLICATIONS (INDIA) LIMITED

G 004 | E 229

First Edition : October, 1994
Revised Edition : October, 1997
Reprint : March 2001

Published by
Navneet Publications (India) Limited

Photographs
Bipin Mistry, Jayant Nayak

Line drawings
Sonali Shail Maniar

Printed at : PRINTMANN, Mumbai 400 013

ISBN 81-243-0662-1

Regd. Office : **Navneet Publications (India) Limited**
Navneet Bhavan, Bhavani Shankar Road, Dadar,
Mumbai – 400 028. Tel. 430 7286 Fax : 437 2568
e-mail: npil@navneet.com
Visit us at: www.navneet.com • www.connectschool.com

Offices:

- **Ahmadabad**
Navneet House, Gurukul Road, Memnagar,
Ahmadabad – 380 052. Tel. 745 1000/745 3995/745 6300
- **Pune**
Sita Park, 18, Shivaji Nagar, Near Bharat English School,
Pune – 411 005. Tel. 553 0401/553 6364
- **Nagpur**
Agge Apartments, Agyaramdevi – S.T. Stand Road,
Nagpur – 440 018. Tel. 72 4411
- **Chennai**
Gala Bhavan, 30 Sriram Nagar, North Street, Alwarpet,
Chennai – 600 018. Tel. 434 6404/433 4145
- **Delhi**
F/6, Bhagat Singh Market, 2nd floor,
New Delhi – 110 001. Tel. 373 3081/334 8404
- **Patna**
5, C/2, Manna Singh Lane, North S.K. Puri,
Behind Rajesh Petrol Pump, Patna-800 013. Tel. 274 152
- **Hyderabad**
Bldg. No. 3-2-331, 2nd floor, Somasundaram Street,
Secunderabad. Tel. C/o 711 5849
- **Bangalore**
No. 98, 1st floor, 6th Cross, 6th Main, Malleswaram,
Bangalore – 560 003. Tel. 346 5740/346 3569
- **Vadodara**
F/1, Vaidya Vatika, Opp. Hanuman Wadi, Sardar Bhuvan Khancho,
Vadodara – 390 001. Tel. (O) (P.P.) 418 648 (R) 564 775

Price : Rs. 80.00

2001 (1)

INTRODUCTION

The recipes introduced in this book have been prepared using wholesome, mostly fresh, and readily available ingredients. Vegetarian food sustains everyone without hurting any living creature, and at the same time it gives pleasure to one and all. There are certain combinations of vegetables, legumes, pulses and grains, that are necessary for sound health. These are harmless alternatives provided by mother nature.

WONDERWORLD OF INDIAN VEGETARIAN CUISINE is a treasure trove of traditional as well as new recipes, which can be used for all occasions. The dishes are satisfying to even the most fastidious palates. The book introduces exciting recipes for the benefit of the urban cook, who prefers to have parties with a buffet-style service. A party can thus start with soup and starters; at the same time, the table can be laid out with puris, curries, sweets and salads.

The recommended quantities given in this book are sufficient for restricted numbers. The same recipes, if made for a buffet party menu, will suffice for 20 servings as the guests at a buffet party usually partake a little of every dish laid out on the table.

This book is not intended to be a low calorie diet book; it is for a healthy normal diet with one special chapter on Healthy Snacks. If one wants to make low calorie dishes, one is at liberty to substitute the ingredients with low fat ingredients without varying most of the basics in the recipe.

Preparation and cooking times have been given to facilitate planning of your busy day. As everyone works at different speeds and with different gadgets, the preparation times given should be used only as a guide.

When recipes are chosen carefully and prepared as per the instructions given in this book, you and your family are certain to enjoy wonderful, wholesome, and satisfying meals every day.

Other books by Jyoti Nikunj Parekh:

- ♣ Wonderworld of Tropical Bonsai
- ♣ Wonderworld of Bonsai and Saikei
- ♣ Wonderworld of Vegetarian Cooking
- ♣ Wonderworld of Gift Wrapping
- ♣ Wonderful Desserts
- ♣ Wonderful Microwave Cooking

ACKNOWLEDGEMENTS

WONDERWORLD OF INDIAN VEGETARIAN CUISINE is a compilation of cookery articles, which appeared regularly in THE HINDU, a renowned newspaper of India, in 1991, 1992 and 1993. The publishers of THE HINDU, requested me from time to time to prepare new, as well as traditional vegetarian recipes for their readers. I am grateful toTHE HINDU, for allowing me to share some of these recipes with the ever-increasing number of vegetarian cuisine lovers all over the world.

I would like to thank my husband NIKUNJ, who constantly inspired me and helped me in every way, including computer typesetting all the recipes. Without his help the production of this book would have been impossible. I would also like to thank my daughter SONALI SHAIL MANIAR for her help with line drawings for this book. I would like to acknowledge and express my appreciation to all the others who have helped me in the preparation of this book, directly or indirectly and whose help has always been forthcoming through the grace of God.

JYOTI NIKUNJ PAREKH

CONTENTS

WEIGHTS & MEASURES

In India, most experienced cooks do not measure all their ingredients exactly while preparing their dishes. Even if they measure, they have their own way of doing so, using bowls or any vessel they are familiar with in daily cooking. But, as the new generation of cooks are venturing into the kitchen, they are more particular about weighing and measuring the ingredients to get accurate results.

Today, a set of scales, measuring jugs and standard measuring cups and spoons, are a must in every modern kitchen. In this book, weights are given in grams (gms.) or kilograms (kgs.) and standard cup measurements. Weighing is more accurate than measuring but for convenience, standard cups and spoons can be used. (For the convenience of the cook, in some of the recipes, the weight in grams is rounded off to the nearest multiple of 25 gms. and 5 gms. depending on the ingredients.)

A standard 8 ounces (ozs.) measuring cup is commonly used for measuring ingredients. Four separate cups of 1/4 cup (2 ozs.), 1/2 cup (4 ozs.), 3/4 cup (6 ozs.) and 1 cup (8 ozs.), are also used depending on an individual's preference. These cups also give measurements in millilitres (mls.) or litres.

Standard teaspoons (tsp.) and tablespoons (tbsp.) should be used for all dishes. Do not use ordinary spoons for measuring because spoon sizes vary with different manufacturers. While measuring the ingredients, always use level measures to avoid errors, unless a recipe specifically indicates using a heaped spoon for an ingredient.

The chart below will help you to follow recipes easily.

1 cup	=	**8 ounces**
2 1/2 cups	=	**1 pint**
1 pint	=	**20 ounces**
1/2 litre	=	**17 ounces**
3 teaspoons	=	**1 tablespoon**
16 tablespoons	=	**1 cup**
1 pound	=	**16 ounces**
1 ounce	=	**30 grams**
1 kilogram	=	**35 ounces**
1 kilogram	=	**2 1/2 pounds**
1 litre	=	**1000 millilitres**

MEASUREMENT GUIDE
ENGLISH, AMERICAN & METRIC

British	American	Metric (approximate)
1 teaspoon	1 teaspoon	5 grams
1 tablespoon	1 tablespoon	14-15 grams
2 tablespoons	3 tablespoons	
3½ tablespoons	4 tablespoons	
4 tablespoons	5 tablespoons	
Solid Measures		
1 lb. butter	2 cups	450 grams
1 lb. flour	4 cups	450 grams
1 lb. sugar	2 cups	410 grams
1 lb. icing sugar	3 cups	375 grams
1 lb. syrup	1 cup	
1 lb. rice	2 cups	400 grams
Liquid Measures		
1 Pint	2½ cups	600 millilitres
1 English teacup	4 fluid ounces	

TEMPERATURE GUIDE

The chart below indicates the oven temperatures in Fahrenheit, Centigrade and Gas numbers. The best guide for understanding oven markings is the booklet supplied by the manufacturer. Also, using the oven frequently for preparing various dishes will enable one to understand how the heat varies in different parts of the oven. For example, the cheese on a pizza placed on the upper shelf of the oven, will melt fast. But when placed on the lower shelf, the base of the pizza will get more crisp.

Oven Temperatures	Temperature Grades		Gas Numbers
	°C	°F	
Slow	50°-100°	225°-230°	¼
Slow moderate	150°	330°	2
Moderate	200°	375°	5
Moderately hot	250°	425°	7
Hot	330°	475°-500°	9

HINDI EQUIVALENTS
OF FRUITS & VEGETABLES

Fig	*Anjeer*
Grapes	*Angoor*
Lime	*Nimbu*
Pomegranate	*Anar*
Sugarmelon	*Shakharteti*
Watermelon	*Kharbuja*
Bottlegourd, White pumpkin	*Lauki*
Brinjal, Eggplant, Aubergine	*Baigan*
Cabbage	*Bandh gobi*
Capsicum, Bell peppers	*Simla mirch, Badi mirch*
Cauliflower	*Phool gobi*
Coriander or Cilantro leaves	*Kothmir*
Fenugreek leaves	*Methi*
French beans	*Fansi*
Mint leaves	*Pudina*
Green peas	*Mattar*
Lettuce	*Salad patta*
Radish	*Mooli*
Red Pumpkin	*Kaddu*
Ridgegourd	*Tori, Turai*
Spinach	*Palak*

HINDI EQUIVALENTS
OF CEREALS, PULSES & LEGUMES

Bengal gram, whole	*Chana*
Bengal gram, whole green	*Hara chana*
Bengal gram, split	*Chana dal*
Bengal gram, flour	*Besan*
Black gram	*Udad*
Black gram, split	*Udad dal*
Corn or maize	*Makkai*
Green gram, whole	*Moong*
Green gram, split with skin	*Moong dal chilkewali*
Green gram, split without skin	*Moong dal*
Kidney beans	*Rajma*
Large white gram, chick peas	*Kabuli chana*
Bengal gram roasted, puffed and split	*Bhuni hui chane ki dal*
Lentil	*Masoor dal*
Millet	*Bajra*
Red gram, split	*Tur dal or Arhar dal*
Rice, pressed	*Poha*
Semolina	*Sooji or Rava*
Vermicelli	*Sevai*
Refined wheat flour	*Maida*

COLD DRINKS

It is the custom to serve a cocktail or a cold drink when guests arrive. Sitting together while sipping drinks creates a relaxed and amicable atmosphere. Moreover, it gives guests time to socialize. One can try various combinations of fruit juices, fruit pieces or aerated drinks to create refreshing drinks.

Vegetable juices are also used to make healthy drinks. If a glass of raw vegetable juice is served, most people will cry out in protest, But experts claim that it is the healthiest drink mother nature offers us. A glass of fresh raw vegetable juice or fruit juice, nourishes the cells and tissues of the body in the speediest and most efficient manner. Why not try various combinations and introduce them to your family a few times a week?

(a brass water jar used during long journeys)

ORANGE MELODY

PREPARATION TIME: 5 MINS. • COOKING TIME: 2 MINS.

MAKES 6 GLASSES

Ingredients

2 cups orange juice
1/2 cup water
1/2 cup ginger juice
3/4 cup sugar
1/4 cup lemon juice
1 cup crushed ice
2 cups chilled water or 1 bottle soda (250 ml.)
A few sprigs mint and slices of orange

Method

1 Prepare the ginger juice by blending the 1A piece of ginger with 1/2 cup of water. Strain the juice.

2 Put the ginger juice, 1/2 cup water and the sugar into a vessel. Place on low heat till the sugar dissolves and then boil. Remove from heat and cool. Mix in the orange juice and lemon juice. Keep chilled.

3 Before serving, fill 1/2 of each glass with Orange Melody. Add crushed ice and fill the rest of the glass with chilled water or soda. Top each glass with a sprig of mint and a slice of orange.

SUDHAMRUT

PREPARATION TIME: OVERNIGHT & 5 MINS. • NO COOKING

MAKES 6 GLASSES

Ingredients

80 black currants
6 teaspoon ani seeds (saunf)
10 almond pieces
6 tablespoons sugar
6 cups water
A few rose petals

Method

1 Soak all the ingredients in 2 cups of water overnight, preferably in a new earthenware pot.

2 Next day, put ingredients into the mixer and extract juice, then strain. Return to the same pot. Add more water and cool.

3 Serve with a rose petal in each glass.

APPLECOLA

PREPARATION TIME: 7 MINS. • NO COOKING

MAKES 6 GLASSES

Ingredients

3 apples, chopped
6 tablespoons demerara sugar (brown sugar)
2 tablespoons lemon juice
1/4 teaspoon cinnamon powder
2 cups crushed ice
4 cups water
A pinch of salt

Method

1 Put the apple pieces, sugar, lemon juice and 1 cup water in a mixer. Blend and strain.

2 Add the crushed ice, water, cinnamon powder, and salt. Serve chilled.

GRAPE COCKTAIL

PREPARATION TIME: 15 MINS. • NO COOKING

MAKES 6 GLASSES

Ingredients

2 cups black grape juice
1 cup orange juice
1 cup carrot juice
2 cups crushed ice
1 teaspoon freshly roasted cummin seeds, powdered
1/4 teaspoon black pepper powder
1/4 teaspoon salt
Sugar to taste
Sprigs of mint to garnish

Method

1 Mix all the ingredients together. Place in the refrigerator till time to serve.

2 Serve in cocktail glasses with a sprig of mint in each glass.

PINK MELODY

PREPARATION TIME: 1 HOUR 10 MINS. • NO COOKING

MAKES 6 GLASSES

Ingredients

4 cups buttermilk
1/2 cup chopped beetroot (small pieces)
1 cup chopped cucumber (small pieces)
1/2 teaspoon black pepper, powdered
1/2 teaspoon freshly roasted cummin seeds, powdered
1/4 teaspoon black salt
2 tablespoons coriander leaves
2 green chillies, split and chopped
3/4 teaspoon salt

Method

1 Prepare buttermilk using the chilled water.

2 Put the beetroot and cucumber pieces along with 2 cups of water, into the mixer. Extract juice and then strain it.

3 Now mix the buttermilk well with all the other ingredients and put the mixture into the refrigerator for at least 1 hour for the flavour to set in.

4 Strain to remove coriander and chillies before serving.

Pink Melody –

To prepare 4 cups of buttermilk, beat 2 1/4 cups of natural yogurt with 1 1/4 cups of chilled water; or buy readymade buttermilk.

Frozen Litchi Ice –

Black grape squash can be used instead of litchi squash to make Frozen Grape Ice.

FROZEN LITCHI ICE

PREPARATION TIME: 45 MINS. • COOKING TIME: 3 MINS.

MAKES 4 GLASSES

Ingredients

1/2 cup litchi squash
1/4 cup lemon juice
2 cups water
1 tablespoon gelatin
4 sprigs mint

Method

1 Using 1/2 cup water, soak the gelatin for 5 minutes. Dissolve it on medium heat. Remove from heat and cool. Add the rest of the water, the litchi squash and lemon juice to the gelatin. Crush the mint leaves roughly to bring out the flavour and mix with the other ingredients.

2 Set in fridge for 1/2 hour. Remove mint leaves. Pour semi-set litchi ice into a divided ice tray and place in the ice compartment. Allow it to freeze.

3 Take out pieces from ice tray. Place a small sprig of mint on top and serve in a glass bowl.

FRUIT PUNCH

PREPARATION TIME: 5 MINS. • COOKING TIME: 15 MINS.

MAKES 4 GLASSES

Ingredients

1 1/2 cups orange juice
1/4 cup chopped orange peel
2 tablespoons lemon juice
1 1/2 cups sweet lime juice
4 blades lemon grass
1 cup hot water
1/4 cup jaggery

Method

1 Place the orange skin and lemon grass in a vessel. Add 1 cup hot water.

2 Cover vessel and set aside for 10 minutes. Strain and add the jaggery. Melt the jaggery and allow the mixture to cool.

3 Mix in the orange, lemon and sweet lime juices.

PINEAPPLE PUNCH

PREPARATION TIME: 5 MINS. • NO COOKING

MAKES 6 GLASSES

Ingredients

- **1 cup pineapple squash**
- **½ cup lemon squash**
- **½ cup fresh cream**
- **½ cup powdered sugar**
- **1 cup crushed ice**
- **3 cups chilled water**
- **A few pineapple pieces**
- **A few glazed cherries**

Method

1 Blend together the pineapple squash, lemon squash, fresh cream, sugar and crushed ice in a blender. Mix in chilled water. Serve chilled on them.

2 Garnish with cocktail sticks with pineapple pieces and cherries on them.

HARIALI

PREPARATION TIME: 5 MINS. • NO COOKING

MAKES 6 GLASSES

Ingredients

- **1½ cups Khus Sherbet**
- **4 bottles aerated lemon drink (300 ml. per bottle)**
- **2 cups crushed ice**
- **A few slices lemon and sprigs of mint**

Method

1 Fill each glass with crushed ice and Khus Sherbet. Add the chilled aerated lemon drink before serving.

2 Top each glass with a slice of lemon and a sprig of mint.

Pineapple Punch–

To make a simple punch, omit the fresh cream and powdered sugar.

Hariali–

A pleasant green coloured khus sherbet is available in Indian grocery stores.

Rosy Refresher –

Coconut milk is prepared by blending grated coconut with double the quantity of warm water. The mixture is drained and the milk squeezed out thoroughly. It is also available readymade in cans.

1 Rosy Refresher p. 6
2 Green Booster p. 6

Colour photo on p. 7

ROSY REFRESHER

PREPARATION TIME: 15 MINS. • NO COOKING

MAKES 4 GLASSES

Ingredients

1 cup tomato juice
$^1/_4$ cup beetroot juice
1 tablespoon raisins – soaked in 1 cup water
1 cup spinach
2 tablespoons lemon juice
3 cups water
Salt to taste

Method

1 Blend and strain the raisin water to remove the skins.
2 Put the tomato and beetroot juice into a vessel. Add the raisin water, coconut milk, salt and sugar. Dilute with $1^1/_4$ cups water.
3 Serve at room temperature or chilled.

GREEN BOOSTER

PREPARATION TIME: 10 MINS. • NO COOKING

MAKES 4 GLASSES

Ingredients

1 cup chopped cucumber (small pieces)
$^1/_2$ cup mint leaves
1 cup coriander leaves
$^1/_2$ cup coconut milk
$1^1/_4$ cups water
Salt and sugar to taste

Method

1 Make a fine paste using the cucumber, mint, coriander and spinach.
2 Add 3 cups water. Mix well and strain.
3 Add the salt and lemon juice.

STARTERS

Along with cold drinks and soups, it is customary to serve mouth-watering snacks. Snacks tickle the palate and build up the appetite. The snacks introduced in this chapter are attractive, often spicy, and small in size to allow for easy handling. They are quick and easy to make, as they are served as side dishes. The dishes in this chapter are light, rather than heavy, so as not to kill the appetite for the main course.

Some recipes in this chapter are for grilled snacks. Grilling food over a charcoal fire is an age-old practice in India. It is now the 'in thing' to serve freshly-prepared, grilled, tasty bites at a party such as spicy, marinated pieces of vegetables and paneer threaded on a skewer and grilled over a fire. The smoky flavour mingles with the spices creating a heavenly aroma. These starters are served hot with chutnies and sauces and are a perfect beginning to an enjoyable evening.

(a bowl-shaped brass stand used for supporting eating bowls and trays)

Chaat Ki Tokri–

(a) To save time, fried chana dal, besan sev and chaat masala can be bought readymade.

(b) Monita's canapés are small square cups with the crispness of wafer biscuits. They can be replaced with any variety of canapés available.

1 **Hariali** p. 5
2 **Pinéapple Punch** p. 5
3 **Chaat Ki Tokri** p. 10
4 **Tirangi Pattice** p. 11

Colour photo on p. 8

CHAAT KI TOKRI
(BASKET CHAAT)

PREPARATION TIME: 3 HOURS 10 MINS. • COOKING TIME: 15 MINS.
MAKES 25 PIECES

Ingredients

25 pieces cocktail canapés (Monita's)
1/2 cup peanuts, boiled in salted water
1/2 cup chana dal
1/2 cup finely chopped onions
1/2 cup chopped coriander leaves
2 green chillies, finely chopped
2 tablespoons lemon juice
2 tablespoons chaat masala
50 gms. fine besan sev
Coriander leaves to garnish
Oil for deep frying

Method

1 Soak the chana dal in water for 3 hours. Drain. Deep fry in oil till crisp.
2 Quick fry the cocktail canapés in hot oil. Cool.
3 Put the boiled peanuts, fried chana dal, onions, green chillies and coriander leaves into a bowl. Add the chaat masala and lemon juice and mix.
4 Before serving, put a tablespoon of chaat in each canapé. Top with fine sev and coriander leaves.

HARE MATAR KE VADE
(GREEN PEAS VADAS)

PREPARATION TIME: OVERNIGHT & 30 MINS.
COOKING TIME: 30 MINS.
MAKES 30 PIECES

Ingredients

5 ozs. urad dal
1/4 teaspoon soda bicarbonate
1 1/2 tablespoons oil
1 cup crushed green peas
2 medium-sized potatoes, boiled and mashed
2 tablespoons chopped coriander leaves
2 tablespoons grated coconut
1/2 tablespoon lemon juice
1/4 teaspoon garam masala
1/2 teaspoon ginger-green chilli paste
A pinch of asafoetida
Oil for frying
Salt to taste

Method

1 Soak the urad dal overnight. Next day, grind to a fine paste. Mix in the asafoetida, a pinch of soda bicarbonate and a little salt. Also add a little water to make the coating consistent. Mix well and set aside.
2 Heat a little oil in a pan. When hot, add crushed peas and a pinch of soda

bicarbonate. Fry, stirring often till peas are cooked. Remove from heat and cool. Add the mashed potatoes, grated coconut, coriander leaves, lemon juice, salt, garam masala and ginger-green chilli paste. Mix everything well and make 30 balls.

3 Now take each ball, dip in the urad dal batter and deep fry till golden brown.

4 Serve hot with Green Coriander Chutney (refer chapter on Pickles, Chutnies & Masalas).

TIRANGI PATTICE
(TRI-COLOURED CHOPS)

PREPARATION TIME: 30 MINS. • COOKING TIME: 30 MINS.
MAKES 30 PIECES

Ingredients

For the white layer

1 kg. potatoes, boiled and mashed
3 tablespoons gram flour
1 tablespoon ginger-green chilli paste
2 tablespoons lemon juice
Salt to taste
2 teaspoons ginger-green chilli paste
1/2 teaspoon sugar
1 tablespoon lemon juice
Salt to taste

For the yellow layer

400 gms. paneer
1/2 teaspoon turmeric powder

For the green layer

1/2 kg. green peas, boiled and mashed
1/2 teaspoon ginger-green chilli paste
Salt to taste

Method

1 Mix the ingredients for all three layers separately. Make 15 balls out of each mixture.

2 Take the yellow paneer ball and cover one portion of it with green peas. Now cover it with white potato mixture. Dip fingers in oil and make the ball into a round smooth pattice.

3 Deep fry till golden brown. After a few minutes cut each pattice into two. Arrange pattice on a serving plate. Serve with tomato ketchup.

Tirangi Pattice

Paneer is readily available in India and is used in savoury as well as sweet dishes. It can also be easily made at home. Boil the milk and curdle it with lemon juice. Drain off the water completely to get paneer.

CHEESE FINGERS

PREPARATION TIME: 15 MINS. • COOKING TIME: 20 MINS.

MAKES 12 PIECES

Ingredients

4 slices of bread
4 tablespoons melted butter
10 tablespoons grated cheese
12 tiny pieces of capsicum
A little tomato ketchup for garnishing

Method

1 Cut each slice of bread into 3 long strips. Roll each one in melted butter. Arrange grated cheese on top of each slice. Make a line of tomato ketchup down the centre. Place a piece of capsicum in the middle.

2 Bake cheese fingers in the oven at 175°C for about 20 minutes till crisp.

HARE CHANE KE KABAB (GREEN GRAM KABABS)

PREPARATION TIME: OVERNIGHT & 30 MINS.

COOKING TIME: 10 MINS.

SERVES 4-6

Ingredients

1 cup green chana (gram)
1 potato, boiled and mashed
1 big onion, grated
2 green chillies, minced
1/2″ ginger, minced
4 cloves garlic, minced
2 tablespoons lemon juice
2 tablespoons gram flour
2 tablespoons finely chopped coriander leaves
Salt to taste

Method

1 Soak the green chana overnight.

2 Next day, cook in a pressure cooker and mash well. Add in all the remaining ingredients. Mix well.

3 Bind mixture onto skewers and roast over charcoal (or in an oven or on a grill) till done.

4 Serve hot with Phudina Chutney and slices of lemon (refer chapter on Pickles, Chutnies & Masalas).

MASALA CHAWAL PAKORA
(SPICY RICE BALLS)

PREPARATION TIME: 10 MINS. • COOKING TIME: 20 MINS.

MAKES 15-20 PIECES

Ingredients

1 cup cooked rice, mashed
$1^1/_4$ cup gram flour
3 slices of bread
3 green chillies, finely chopped
3 tablespoons coriander leaves
$^1/_2$ teaspoon cummin seeds
1 tablespoon amchoor powder (dry mango powder)
$^1/_4$ teaspoon turmeric powder
2 tablespoons oil
2 tablespoons grated cheese
Salt to taste

For the garlic chutney

20 cloves garlic
2 teaspoons red chilli powder
2 tablespoons lemon juice
1 teaspoon salt

Method

1 Soak the bread slices in a little water. Squeeze and mix with the mashed rice. Add the gram flour, green chillies, coriander leaves, amchoor powder, turmeric powder, salt and grated cheese.
2 Heat the oil and add the cummin seeds. Fry till brown. Add in the prepared mixture. Mix well and retain over heat till warm. Cool and make balls. Push the balls onto skewers and roast on charcoal or on a grill. Serve hot with Garlic Chutney.

For the Garlic Chutney
Take all the ingredients in a blender and make into a paste. Add a little water to adjust the consistency.

PANEER BISCUITS
(COTTAGE CHEESE CRACKERS)

PREPARATION TIME: 15 MINS. • COOKING TIME: 20 MINS.

MAKES 12 PIECES

Ingredients

12 cream cracker biscuits
10 tablespoons crumbled paneer
1 onion, finely chopped
1 green chilli, finely chopped
2 tablespoons chopped coriander leaves
2 tablespoons oil
Salt to taste

Method

1 Heat the oil and sauté the onions and chillies till soft. Add the paneer crumbs, salt and $^3/_4$ of the coriander leaves. Mix well and cook till soft. Remove from heat.

Masala Chawal Pakora–

Rice balls can be deep fried or grilled.

2 Arrange the mixture evenly on the cream cracker biscuits. Garnish each one with coriander leaves and serve.

PANEER TIKKI
(COTTAGE CHEESE CAKES)

PREPARATION TIME: 10 MINS. • COOKING TIME: 15 MINS.

MAKES 20 PIECES

Ingredients

250 gms. paneer cut into 1/2" squares
1 cup gram flour
2 tablespoons wheat flour
1/4 teaspoon soda bicarbonate
1/4 teaspoon garam masala
1 teaspoon anardana (dry pomegranate seed) powder
1 teaspoon amchoor (dry mango powder)
1 teaspoon ginger-green chilli paste
1/4 teaspoon garam masala
1/4 teaspoon turmeric powder
Oil to deep fry
Salt to taste

Method

1 Mix all the seasonings with the gram flour and then add the wheat flour. Add water to make a thick batter. Dip each piece of paneer in the batter and deep fry in oil.

2 Serve hot with Green Coriander Chutney or tomato ketchup (refer chapter on Pickles, Chutnies & Masalas).

PALAK PANEER TIKKI
(SPINACH AND COTTAGE CHEESE CAKES)

PREPARATION TIME: 2 HOURS 10 MINS. • COOKING TIME: 30 MINS.

MAKES 20-25 PIECES

Ingredients

1/4 kg. paneer pieces
1/4 cup palak (spinach) paste
3 green chillies, minced
3 tablespoons curd
1/2 teaspoon freshly roasted cummin seeds, powdered
1/4 teaspoon black salt
1/4 teaspoon garam masala
2 tablespoons ghee or oil
A few slices of onion
A few slices of lemon
Salt to taste

Method

1 Mix the palak paste, green chillies, curd, ghee and spices together. Marinate the paneer pieces in it for 2 hours.

2 Arrange the pieces on a greased baking tray. Bake at 200°C in a moderate oven till dry. Turn the pieces when half done. Leave them to turn light brown. Serve hot with onion rings and lemon slices.

TANDOORI BITES

PREPARATION TIME: 2 HOURS 15 MINS.
COOKING TIME: 10 MINS.
SERVES 4-6

Ingredients

1/4 kg. paneer, (big pieces)
2 capsicums, cut into big pieces
2 onions, cut into big pieces
10 mushrooms

For the marinade

1 cup curd
1/4 teaspoon black pepper powder
1/2 teaspoon garam masala
2 tablespoons lemon juice
Tandoori colouring as required
2 tablespoons oil
Salt to taste

Method

1 Mix all the ingredients together for the marinade. Take the prepared paneer and vegetable pieces and mix well. Set aside for about 2 hours.
2 Take the pieces and push onto skewers. Grill on charcoal, in an oven, or on a grill. Cook till done. Serve hot.

PANEER HERB BALLS

PREPARATION TIME: 1 HOUR 15 MINS. • NO COOKING
MAKES 20 PIECES

Ingredients

3/4 cup paneer crumbs
1/4 cup grated processed cheese
1 tablespoon dill (suwa bhaji), finely chopped
2 tablespoons thick cream
1 teaspoon ginger-green chilli paste
2 tablespoons bread crumbs
1/2 teaspoon salt

Method

1 Put the paneer crumbs, cheese, cream, ginger-green chilli paste and salt in a mixer jar and blend well. Remove the mixture onto a plate and mix in the dill evenly.
2 Make 20 balls and roll them evenly in bread crumbs. Chill them in the refrigerator.
3 Push a toothpick into each ball and serve.

OR

Place the prepared mixture on a sheet of aluminium foil. Sprinkle the bread crumbs and make into a 9-inch-long roll. Cover with foil and chill this roll in the refrigerator. Open the foil casing and cut into slices before serving. Put each slice on a salty biscuit and serve.

Paneer Herb Balls –

The thick cream required in the recipe can be bought readymade or taken from the top of skimmed milk.

HEALTHY SNACKS

(a metal steam cooker)

Traditionally, snacks are served with evening tea. These snacks can be fried, roasted or grilled. Children too, enjoy snacks, especially when their growing bodies need extra food in-between meals. Instead of giving them readymade snacks, health-conscious parents can serve some of the recipes introduced in this chapter, which are easy to make and nutritious, but more importantly, not deep fried. Parents can confidently pack some of these snacks in their children's lunch boxes for their light mid-day meals. Some of these recipes can be served as a single-dish meal and are ideal for a light and satisfying dinner.

CHAWAL SEVAI KI UPMA
(RICE VERMICELLI UPMA)

PREPARATION TIME: 15 MINS. • COOKING TIME: 15 MINS.
SERVES 8

Ingredients

- 1 packet Instant Rice Sevai – 200 gms.
- 4 tablespoons oil
- 1 teaspoon cummin seeds
- 4 green chillies, chopped
- 3/4 cup chopped onions
- 1/4 cup chopped coriander leaves
- 1 cup chopped and boiled mixture of French beans, carrots, green peas
- 1/4 cup grated coconut
- 1/4 cup lemon juice
- 1 tablespoon powdered sugar
- A few curry leaves
- Salt to taste

Method

1 Cook the instant rice sevai according to the instructions on the packet.

2 Heat the oil in a vessel. Add the cummin seeds and after 1/2 minute, add the green chillies and curry leaves. After another 1/2 minute, add the onions and sauté till they turn soft and light pink in colour.

3 Add the sevai, vegetables, lemon juice, sugar and salt. Mix well. Finally, add the coriander leaves and coconut and stir. Serve hot with Green Coriander Chutney (refer to chapter on Pickles, Chutnies & Masalas).

SUKHE NARIYAL KI CHAAT
(DRY COCONUT CHAAT)

PREPARATION TIME: 30 MINS. • NO COOKING
SERVES 6

Ingredients

- 1 cup well-sprouted moong (green gram)
- 1/2 cup chopped cucumber
- 1/2 cup chopped tomatoes
- 1/4 cup chopped onions
- 1/2 cup boiled and chopped potatoes
- 1 1/2 cups-curd, beaten
- Chaat masala to taste
- A few coriander leaves, chopped

For the dry coconut masala

- 1/4 cup grated dry coconut, lightly roasted
- 1/4 cup peanuts, roasted and coarsely ground
- 1/2 tablespoon sesame seeds
- 1/2 tablespoon poppy seeds
- 1 teaspoon ginger-green chilli paste
- 1 tablespoon lemon juice
- Salt to taste

Method

1 Arrange the sprouted moong and vegetables in layers. Sprinkle chaat masala over the arrangement.

2 Beat the curd with a little salt. Pour it evenly over the chaat.

3 Sprinkle the dry coconut masala mixture and coriander leaves over the top.

Rice Vermicelli Upma–

Rice Sevai is similar to thin noodles made from rice flour.

RAWA IDLI

PREPARATION TIME: 20 MINS. • COOKING TIME: 40 MINS.

MAKES 16 PIECES

Ingredients

For the idlis

1 cup semolina
3 tablespoons ghee
1/4 teaspoon soda bicarbonate
3 green chillies, chopped
1/4 cup cashewnut pieces
A few curry leaves
1/4 cup chopped coriander leaves
1/4 cup grated fresh coconut
1 1/2 cups fresh curd
A little oil for greasing
Salt to taste

For the red coconut chutney

1/2 cup chopped onions
1/2 cup chopped tomatoes
1/2 cup grated coconut
1/4 cup oil
1/4 cup curd
2 teaspoons red chilli powder
Salt to taste

Method

For the Rawa Idlis

1 Take a teaspoon of ghee in a vessel. Sauté the cashewnut pieces in this till they are a light pink in colour. Remove and set aside.

2 Add the remaining ghee to the same vessel and melt. Add the green chillies and curry leaves. Sauté for a minute. Add the semolina and sauté till it turns a very light pink. Stir continuously. Remove from heat and cool to room temperature.

3 Add the soda bicarbonate, salt, cashewnut pieces, coriander leaves, coconut and fresh curd. Mix well and allow the mixture to soak for 10 minutes.

4 Boil 2 cups of water in a flat, deep vessel. Place a metal ring in the centre. Put a plate on it which can hold 6 metal cups for steaming the idlis. Cover the vessel tightly.

5 Grease 6 metal cups with a little oil. Put about 2 tablespoons of the idli mixture into each. Place the cups in the prepared vessel for steaming. Steam for 8-10 minutes. Remove the cups from the steaming vessel. Cool for 5 minutes. Take the idlis out carefully with a spoon. Use the same method to make the remaining idlis. Serve hot with Red Coconut Chutney.

For the Red Coconut Chutney

1 Sauté the onions in oil. When light pink in colour, remove from heat and cool.

2 Put the rest of the ingredients and the saute'ed onions into a mixer and make the chutney.

SIMLA MIRCH SAMOSE
(CAPSICUM SAMOSAS)

PREPARATION TIME: 45 MINS. • COOKING TIME: 1 HOUR

MAKES 24 PIECES

Ingredients

For the covering

2 cups flour
1 teaspoon baking powder
3/4 cup spinach paste
3 green chillies, chopped
4 tablespoons oil
1/2 teaspoon salt
Oil for deep frying

For the stuffing

2 cups boiled and chopped potatoes
1 cup green peas, boiled
6 green chillies, finely chopped
1/2″ ginger, minced
1/2 teaspoon garam masala
2 tablespoons amchoor (dry mango powder)
1/4 cup chopped coriander leaves
2 tablespoons oil
Salt to taste

Method

For the stuffing

Heat the oil and add in all the ingredients. Mix well and then remove from heat. Cool to room temperature.

For the covering

1 Mix all the ingredients for the covering and add just enough water to make a tight dough. Knead well and make 12 balls.
2 Roll each ball of dough into a 5″ diameter round; then cut into two. Fold each semi-circle into a cone shape; fill it with the prepared stuffing. Seal the sides adequately and collect together the dough on the upper part. Each samosa should have the shape of a whole capsicum.
3 Arrange all the samosas in a greased baking tray. Bake at 250°C for 20 minutes. Then reduce temperature to 150°C and bake for another 30 minutes. Serve hot with tomato ketchup.

HARI IDLI DAHIWALI
(GREEN IDLIS WITH CURD)

PREPARATION TIME: 15 MINS. • COOKING TIME: 30 MINS.

SERVES 6-8

Ingredients

1 packet readymade idli mix – 200 gms.
1 cup chopped spinach
3 green chillies
Salt to taste
2 cups curd, beaten
3 tablespoons oil
1 teaspoon mustard seeds
½ teaspoon cummin seeds
2 green chillies, chopped
¼ cup chopped coriander leaves
A few curry leaves

Method

1 Make a paste with the spinach and 3 green chillies. Add it to the idli mix and soak according to the instructions on the packet but with a little less water. Add a little extra salt for the spinach.
2 Steam the green idlis in a mini idli mould.
3 Beat the curd with a little salt. Place the mini idlis on a serving plate. Pour the curd evenly over them.
4 Heat oil; add the mustard seeds and cummin seeds. When they stop sputtering, add the green chillies and curry leaves. After ½ minute pour this over the idlis covered with curd. Sprinkle coriander leaves over the lot. Prepare this dish at least 15 minutes before it is time to serve.

MASALA DAL PANKU
(SPICY DAL PANKU)

PREPARATION TIME: 12 HOURS 25 MINS.
COOKING TIME: 30 MINS.
MAKES 20 PIECES

Ingredients

1 cup moong dal (green gram split)
½ cup chana dal (Bengal gram split)
¼ cup udad dal (black gram split)
¼ cup chopped and boiled French beans
¼ cup chopped and boiled carrots
¼ teaspoon soda bicarbonate
¼ teaspoon tumeric powder
1 tablespoon ginger-green chilli paste
3 tablespoons oil
A big pinch of asafoetida
Salt to taste
Oil for shallow frying

For the topping

⅓ cup sprouted Moong (Green gram)
½ cup finely chopped tomatoes
½ cup finely chopped onion
¼ cup chopped coriander leaves
3 green chillies, finely chopped
Chaat masala to taste

Method

1 Soak the dals for at least 6 hours. Grind to a paste. Mix the soda-bicarbonate and beat well. Cover and set aside in a closed, warm place to ferment for 6 hours.
2 Add all the spices, French beans, carrots and a little water to the fermented dals to make a spreading consistency.
3 In a flat non-stick griddle, heat a little oil. Make small rounds with the batter. Sprinkle on some of the topping. Allow the bottom of the Panku to become crisp and turn a light-brown colour. Flip over and cook for another minute. Serve hot with tomato ketchup or Green Coriander Chutney (refer to chapter on Pickles, Chutnies & Masalas).

1 Sabzi Dahi Chilka p. 22

Colour photo on p. 26

SABZI DAHI CHILKA (VEGETABLE CURD PANCAKES)

PREPARATION TIME: 30 MINS. • COOKING TIME: 30 MINS.

MAKES 20 PIECES

Ingredients

For the pancakes

1/2 cup grated potatoes
1/2 cup grated carrots
1/4 cup grated onion
1/4 cup chopped coriander leaves
1/4 teaspoon baking powder
6 cloves garlic, minced
3-4 green chillies, chopped
1 cup curd
1 cup semolina
1 teaspoon cummin seeds
Salt to taste
Oil for shallow frying

For the curd sauce

1 cup thick curd
2 tablespoons tomato ketchup
1 teaspoon chilli sauce
1 tablespoon finely chopped coriander leaves
3 mint leaves, finely chopped
Salt to taste

Method

For the pancakes

1 Mix all the ingredients for the pancakes and set aside for 15 minutes.

2 Make small pancakes using a little oil on a flat non-stick griddle. They should turn light brown on both sides. Serve hot with the curd sauce.

For the curd sauce

1 Put the curd in a fine sieve. Set aside for more than 1 hour till the water drains out completely and only 1/2 cup thick curd remains.

2 Add the rest of the ingredients to the thick curd. Keep the sauce chilled till you wish to serve.

JOWAR-BAJRA CHAAT
(Millet Chaat)

PREPARATION TIME: 7 HOURS • COOKING TIME: 45 MINS.
SERVES 6

Ingredients

$^1/_2$ cup jowar (white millet)
$^3/_4$ cup bajra (millet)
2 tablespoons oil
6 spring onions with tender green leaves, chopped
$^3/_4$ cup chopped tomatoes
2-3 green chillies, chopped
Chaat masala to taste
$1^1/_2$ cups curd, beaten
6 tablespoons Sweet and Sour Chutney
3 tablespoons Green Tomato Chutney
A few coriander leaves, chopped
$^1/_2$ cup roasted masala poha (beaten rice)

Method

For the pancakes

1 Soak the jowar and bajra for at least 6 hours. Pressure cook with a little salt. Drain off the excess water.

2 Heat the oil in a pan and add the spring onions and green chillies. Sauté for a minute. Add the tomatoes, salt and 2 teaspoons of chaat masala. Add in the jowar and bajra. Mix well and remove from heat.

For the masala poha

3 Take $^1/_2$ cup poha and roast over medium heat till crisp. Add a pinch of turmeric powder, $^1/_4$ teaspoon red chilli powder and salt to taste.

To assemble the chaat

4 Take one portion of the jowar-bajra mixture in a serving bowl. Pour the beaten curd, with little salt, over it. Sprinkle in the masala poha, then put in the Sweet and Sour Chutney, Green Tomato Chutney and Chaat masala. Sprinkle coriander leaves over the Chaat and serve.

Jowar-Bajra Chaat–

For both the chutnies and the Chaat masala, refer to the chapter Pickles, Chutnies & Masalas.

1 Tandoori Bites p. 15

Colour photo on p. 25

SOUPS

(a double ewer used for carrying water and other liquids)

Soups are an important part of a menu. Whether at a party, a family meal or on a special occasion, soups introduce the food that is to follow. They should be pleasing in taste and attractive in appearance and texture. Moreover, their flavours should be strong and aromatic enough to awaken the appetites of the most fastidious eater. There are many varieties of soups –thin, clear, creamy, thick, hot or cold. A thin, light soup can be served with a large, hearty dinner and a thick, nutritious soup with a simple, light meal.

Soups should be garnished to make them aesthetically appealing and can be served attractively in bowls or deep plates. Sprinkle grated cheese or freshly crushed or chopped herbs and a slice of lemon; float croutons; add a swirl of cream or thinly beaten fresh curd, for a touch of sophistication.

C
D
D

EXOTIC TRI-COLOUR SOUP

PREPARATION TIME: 30 MINS. • COOKING TIME: 30 MINS.

SERVES 6

Ingredients

For the red creamy soup

- **3/4 kg tomatoes**
- **1 carrot**
- **1 small beetroot**
- **1 onion**
- **3-4 cloves garlic**
- **1 1/2 tablespoons butter**
- **1 tablespoon flour**
- **3/4 cup milk**
- **Salt, pepper, and sugar to taste**

For the green creamy soup

- **5 cups chopped spinach**
- **1 onion, chopped**
- **2-3 cloves**
- **1 1/2 tablespoons butter**
- **1 1/2 tablespoons flour**
- **3/4 cup milk**
- **Salt and pepper to taste**

For the white colour

- **6 tablespoons fresh cream**

Method

For the red creamy soup

1 Cut the vegetables into big pieces and pressure cook with a little water. Cool and make into a purée.

2 Melt the butter and add in the flour and stir for a minute. Add the milk and stir till it becomes sauce-like. Mix in the vegetable purée, salt, pepper and sugar. Adjust the water content to make 6 servings.

3 Simmer for 10 minutes. Strain this soup to get a smooth creamy consistency.

For the green creamy soup

1 Cook the spinach and make into a purée. Melt the butter. Add the onion and cloves and sauté till the onions turn soft. Add the spinach paste and about 4 cups of water. Bring to a boil. Dissolve the flour in the milk and add to the boiling soup. Add salt and pepper to taste. Strain the soup and discard the cloves. Strain this soup to get a smooth creamy consistency.

2 For serving, gently pour the red creamy soup from one side of the bowl and the green creamy soup from the other side of the bowl, both occupying equal space.

3 Take fresh cream and beat it slightly till it thickens. Make a ring of cream in the centre of the bowl and serve this exotic tricolour soup immediately.

1 Cheese Fingers p.12
2 Exotic Tri-colour Soup p. 29

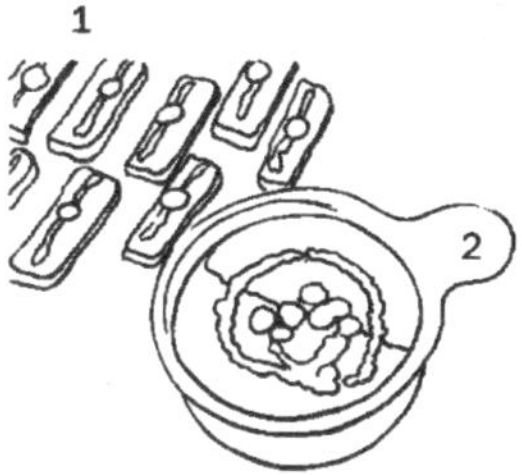

Colour photo on p. 27

---

1 Vegetable Salad Supreme p. 37
2 Vegetable Ring Salad p. 36
3 Cucumber Curd Tower p. 35

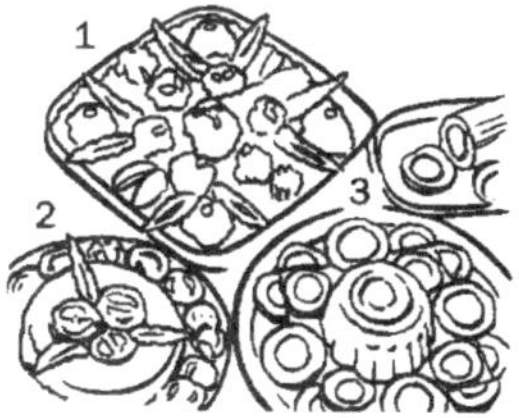

Colour photo on p. 28

Coconut Bean Pot Soup–

To make croutons, toast slices of bread and cut 1/2" squares. Shallow fry in butter till golden brown. Garlic flavored croutons can be made by sprinkling a little garlic salt on the bread before shallow frying.

Apple Soup–

Use the hard and sour variety of apples for this soup.

COCONUT BEAN POT SOUP

PREPARATION TIME: 6 HOURS 10 MINS.
COOKING TIME: 20 MINS.
SERVES 6

Ingredients

1 tablespoon Rajma (kidney beans)
1 tablespoon Chola (black eyed beans)
1 tablespoon Chana dal (Bengal gram split)
1 1/2 cups tomato juice
1 cup coconut milk
1 tablespoon butter
A few bread croutons
Salt-Pepper to taste

Method

1 Soak the rajma, chola and chana dals for 6 hours. Add 2 cups of water and pressure cook. Cool and make into a pureé.

2 Melt the butter and add the prepared pureé, tomato juice, coconut milk and salt and pepper to taste. Adjust the water content to get the right consistency for the soup. Bring to a boil and then simmer for 10 minutes. Serve hot with a few bread croutons floating in each bowl.

APPLE SOUP

PREPARATION TIME: 10 MINS. • COOKING TIME: 20 MINS.
SERVES 6

Ingredients

2 apples, chopped
2 tablespoons butter
2 tablespoons demerara sugar
1/2 cup grated carrot
1/2 cup milk
1 1/2 tablespoons flour
1 tablespoon lemon juice
A big pinch of cinnamon powder
A few sprigs of mint
Salt to taste

Method

1 Melt the butter and add in the chopped apples and demerara sugar. Sauté for a few minutes. Add 6 cups of water and boil till the apples are cooked. Cool and make into a pureé. Put the pureé back on the stove and mix in the grated carrot.

2 Mix the flour and milk evenly and add it to the apple pureé. Add the salt, lemon juice and cinnamon powder. Mix well and simmer for 10 minutes for the flavours to set in. Serve hot with a sprig of mint in each bowl.

CORN CHOWDER

PREPARATION TIME: 10 MINS. • COOKING TIME: 20 MINS.

SERVES 6

Ingredients

2 cups fresh corn
2 tablespoons butter
1 medium onion, chopped
3-4 garlic cloves, chopped
6 button mushrooms (optional)
½ cup milk
1 tablespoon corn meal or corn flour
Grated cheese to garnish
Salt-Pepper to taste

Method

1 Pressure cook the corn with a little water. Cool and make into a purée.
2 Melt the butter and add the onions, garlic and mushrooms. Sauté on a low flame till they turn soft. Add the corn purée.
3 Mix the corn meal and milk evenly and add to the soup. Adjust the water content to make 6 cups. Add salt and pepper to taste. Simmer for a few minutes. Serve hot with a spoonful of grated cheese sprinkled over each bowl.

TADKA DAL SOUP

PREPARATION TIME: 5 MINS. • COOKING TIME: 30 MINS.

SERVES 6

Ingredients

½ cup tur dal (red gram split)
2 cups tomato juice
2 tablespoons oil
1 teaspoon cummin seeds
2 cloves
2 small pieces of cinnamon
1 green chilli, cut into long pieces
A few lemon slices
Salt to taste

Method

1 Wash and pressure cook the tur dal. Remove the dal and add 4 cups of water. Mix lightly and then allow it to settle for 15 minutes. Pour off the dal water into a separate pan to make the soup. Use the dal for some other recipe.
2 Add the tomato juice and salt to the dal water. Return to the stove and simmer over gentle heat.
3 Prepare the *tadka* by heating the oil and adding in the cummin seeds, cinnamon and cloves. When they start sputtering, add the chilli pieces and stir for ½ minute; add this to the soup.
4 Allow the soup to simmer for 15 minutes for the flavours to set in. Serve with slices of lemon.

CURRIED VEGETABLE SOUP

PREPARATION TIME: 10 MINS. • COOKING TIME: 30 MINS.

SERVES 6

Ingredients

2 tablespoons butter
1 onion, chopped
2 teaspoons curry powder
1/2 teaspoon ginger, minced
2 cups water
1/4 cup rice
1 cup cauliflower pieces
1/2 cup cabbage pieces
1/2 cup potato pieces
1/4 teaspoon black pepper powder
1/2 cup tomato juice
A few garlic bread croutons
Salt-Pepper to taste

Method

1 Sauté the onions in the melted butter for a few minutes. Stir in the curry powder, ginger, rice and vegetables. Sauté for a few minutes, stirring occasionally. When the vegetable pieces look soft, add in the water. Adjust heat to simmer gently. Cover and cook for 20 minutes. Add salt and pepper.

2 Mix the vegetables in a blender. Sieve and then return to the stove.

3 Add the tomato juice and more water to adjust the consistency. Bring to a boil. Add a few garlic bread croutons to each bowl. Serve hot.

MINT DAL SOUP

PREPARATION TIME: 2 HOURS 10 MINS.

COOKING TIME: 20 MINS.

SERVES 6

Ingredients

1/4 cup moong dal (green gram split without skin)
1/4 cup masoor dal (lentil)
2 tablespoons butter
1 big onion, chopped
3 cloves garlic, chopped
1 cup grated carrot
3 sprigs of mint
2 cups vegetable stock (made from cabbage, onion and potato)
1/4 teaspoon black pepper
1/2 cup thick curd
Salt to taste

Method

1 Soak the moong and masoor dals for 2 hours.

2 Cut the cabbage, onion and potato into big pieces. Add 2 cups water and pressure cook. Drain off the water and use it as vegetable stock.

3 Melt the butter and fry the onion and garlic in it for a minute. Add the carrot and both the dals; fry for a few more

minutes. Add the vegetable stock and the mint. Bring to a boil and simmer till both the dals are cooked.

4 Remove the mint leaves. Purée the cooked soup and return to the stove. Add the salt and black pepper. Add water to adjust the consistency. Bring to a boil. Serve with a spoonful of thick curd added to each bowl along with a fresh sprig of mint.

SPLIT PEA SOUP

PREPARATION TIME: 20 MINS. • COOKING TIME: 1 HOUR

SERVES 6

Ingredients

1 tablespoon butter or ghee
1/2 cup chopped onions
1 teaspoon minced garlic and ginger
2 teaspoons cummin and coriander seeds powder
1/4 teaspoon tumeric powder
2 green chillies, split and chopped
6 cups water
1/2 cup dried green or yellow split peas
1 Bay leaf
1 cup finely chopped cauliflower and carrot
1 tablespoon chopped coriander leaves
2 tablespoons lemon juice or 1/4 cup thick curd
Salt to taste

Method

1 In a large heavy vessel, melt the butter over moderate heat. Add the onions; cover and cook, stirring occasionally, for 5 minutes. Add the garlic, ginger, cummin-coriander powder, turmeric and green chillies. Cook for 1 more minute.

2 Add the water, washed split peas, Bay leaf and salt. Bring to a boil. Adjust heat to simmer gently. Cover and cook for about 30 minutes till the peas are cooked. Remove the Bay leaf.

3 Blend the mixture to make a fine purée. Return the purée to the same vessel and bring to a boil. Now add the cauliflower and carrot pieces. Simmer till the vegetables are tender. Add the lemon juice or curd, coriander leaves and enough water to get the right consistency for the soup. Serve hot.

Split Pea Soup –

(a) The use of butter or ghee neutralizes the smell of the peas and cauliflower.
(b) The use of freshly roasted cummin powder is preferred in this recipe.

SALADS

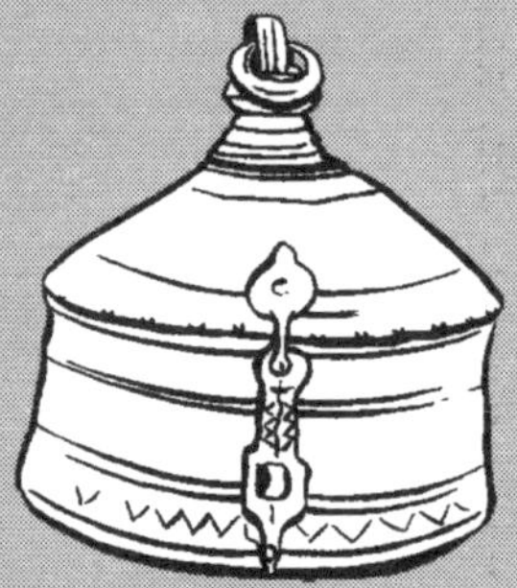

(a metal box used for storing dried dates and nuts)

Who can resist a fresh, crunchy salad? A platter full of your favourite vegetables and fruits with a dash of choice dressing is a real treat. One can capture beauty, vitality and goodness in a bowl of salad.

Some salads can be made additionally appetizing by setting them in fancy moulds. Garnishing them with crisp vegetables and carved vegetable and fruit decorations can make salads look extremely attractive and colourful.

It is customary in India to serve a small quantity of salad with each meal. These are known as *raitas* and *kachumber*. They are served along with a chutney and a pickle in every *thali* (a round plate in which the meal is served).

CUCUMBER CURD TOWER

PREPARATION TIME: 20 MINS.
COOKING TIME: 2 HOURS 30 MINS.
SERVES 10-12

Ingredients

For the cucumber stuffing

- 2 big cucumbers, about 8″ long
- 1 cup paneer, finely mashed
- 2 tablespoons thick fresh cream
- 3 tablespoons dessicated coconut
- 1 tablespoon lemon juice
- 1 tablespoon powdered sugar
- A few drops of yellow colouring
- Salt to taste

For the curd tower

- 2 tablespoons gelatin
- 1/2 cup water
- 2 cups thick curd
- 1/2 cup grated cucumber
- Salt and pepper to taste

Method

For the cucumber stuffing

1 Peel the cucumber only if the skin is tough. Carefully scoop out the entire soft seedy portion from the centre of each cucumber with the help of a penknife and use the back of a spoon to make a hollow.

2 Prepare the stuffing by mixing together the paneer crumbs, fresh cream, coconut, salt, lemon juice and powdered sugar.

3 Divide the stuffing into 2 parts. Mix a few drops of yellow colouring to 1/2 of the mixture. Put the yellow stuffing into one cucumber and the white stuffing in the other one. Chill the cucumbers; later cut into slices and leave them in the refrigerator. Arrange around the salad mould just before you wish to serve.

For the curd tower

1 Soak the gelatin in 1/2 cup water for 5 minutes and then dissolve over low heat.

2 Add the melted gelatin into a mixture of curd, grated cucumber, salt and pepper. Mix evenly and pour into a tall wet jelly mould. Place in the refrigerator till firmly set.

3 Unmould onto a serving plate. Leave in the refrigerator till time to serve. Decorate with the stuffed cucumber slices.

VEGETABLE RING SALAD

PREPARATION TIME: 30 MINS.
COOKING TIME: 2 HOURS 15 MINS.
SERVES 10-12

Ingredients

1/2 cup chopped French beans
1/2 cup chopped carrot
1/2 cup peas, boiled
2 green chillies, chopped
2 tablespoons chopped coriander leaves
1 1/2 tablespoons gelatin
3/4 cup vegetable stock
1 cup curd sauce
1/2 teaspoon salt
Salad leaves, tomatoes and beetroot for decoration

For the curd sauce

3/4 cup curd, with water drained off
1/4 cup cream
1 tablespoon powdered sugar
1/4 teaspoon black pepper powder
1/4 teaspoon mustard paste or powder
1 tablespoon oil
1/2 teaspoon salt

Method

For the vegetable ring

1. Boil the French beans and carrots with a little salt in 1 1/2 cups water. When they are cooked, drain and save the stock.
2. Dissolve the gelatin in the vegetable stock; add it to the curd sauce and mix well. Put it in the refrigerator to semi-set.
3. Mix in the boiled vegetables, chillies, coriander leaves and salt with the semi-set curd sauce.
4. Pour the mixture into a ring mould and refrigerate.
5. Unmould onto a serving plate and fill the centre with small pieces of beetroot and cucumber. Decorate with tomatoes, salad leaves and beetroot.

For the curd sauce

Mix the curd and cream together; beat till you get a smooth consistency. Add the rest of the ingredients and mix well. Use as required. This sauce can be preserved in the refrigerator for a few days.

CREAMY BEAN SALAD

PREPARATION TIME: 12 HOURS & 15 MINS.
COOKING TIME: 20 MINS.
SERVES 10-12

Ingredients

For the salad

1 cup boiled and cubed potatoes
1 cup chickpeas (kabuli chana)
1/4 teaspoon soda bicarbonate
1/2 tin baked beans in tomato sauce (200 gms.)
1 cup chopped spinach
1 onion, finely chopped
1 tomato, finely chopped
1 capsicum, finely chopped
Bean sauce, as required
1/2 teaspoon salt

For the bean sauce

2 tablespoons oil
1/2 tin baked beans in tomato sauce (200 gms.)
1/2 cup fresh curd
1 teaspoon red chilli powder
1/2 teaspoon black pepper powder
Tomatoes, capsicum, and lettuce for garnishing
1/2 teaspoon salt

Method

1 Soak the chickpeas in water for 12 hours and then pressure cook with the salt and soda bicarbonate. Drain off the water.

2 Prepare the bean sauce by blending all the ingredients for the sauce in a blender. Mix all the vegetables for the salad with the bean sauce.

3 Remove into a serving bowl. Garnish with tomatoes, capsicum and lettuce.

VEGETABLE SALAD SUPREME

PREPARATION TIME: 30 MINS. • COOKING TIME: 45 MINS.
SERVES 10-12

Ingredients

1 cup boiled and chopped potatoes
1/2 cup boiled and chopped carrot
1/2 cup boiled and chopped French beans
1/2 cup green peas, boiled
1/2 cup chopped onions
1/2 cup chopped pineapple

For the sauce coating

1 cup milk
2 cloves
1 tablespoon chopped onion
2 tablespoons chopped carrot
6 peppercorns
2 pieces mace
1 1/2 tablespoons margarine or butter
1 tablespoon flour

Curd sauce to bind (refer recipe of Cucumber Curd Tower page)
Salt and pepper to taste
3 tablespoons curd sauce
Salad leaves, glaze cherries and green peels for decoration
Salt to taste

Method

For the salad

1 Prepare the salad by mixing together all the vegetables, curd sauce, salt and pepper. Arrange in small rounds on a serving plate as shown in the picture.

For the sauce coating

2 Boil the milk with the cloves, onion, carrot, peppercorn and salt, for a few minutes. Strain the milk and discard the vegetables and spices.
3 Melt the margarine and add the flour, stirring for a minute. Add the prepared milk, stirring continuously till it reaches a sauce-like consistency. Remove from the stove and cool. Mix the curd sauce and salt. Use for coating the salad rounds.
4 Decorate with salad leaves, glaze cherries and green peels.

VITAMIN SALAD

PREPARATION TIME: 20 MINS. • COOKING TIME: 10 MINS.

SERVES 6

Ingredients

1 tablespoon oil
2 tablespoons lemon juice
½ cup raw papaya pieces
½ cup carrot pieces
½ cup guava pieces (preferably the pink variety)
½ cup cucumber pieces
½ cup bedana pomegranate (soft seeded)
½ cup chopped coriander leaves
Salt to taste
Guava and cucumber slices for decoration

Method

1 Heat the oil and add the pieces of raw papaya and carrot. Stir well and leave on the stove for a few minutes, till the papaya and carrot pieces are soft but crisp. Remove from heat and cool.
2 Mix in the guava, cucumber, pomegranate, salt, lemon juice and coriander leaves.
3 Serve in a bowl decorated with guava and cucumber slices.

CRISP RAW PAPAYA SALAD

PREPARATION TIME: 10 MINS. • COOKING TIME: 7 MINS.

SERVES 6

Ingredients

2 cups grated raw papaya
$1/2$ teaspoon turmeric powder
$1/4$ cup dalia, coarsely powdered
2 tablespoons chopped coriander leaves
2 tablespoons grated coconut
2 tablespoons lemon juice
Salt to taste

For tempering

2 tablespoons oil
1 teaspoon mustard seeds
1 green chilli, split and cut into big pieces

Method

1 Apply salt and turmeric powder to the grated papaya and set aside for at least 15 minutes. Lightly squeeze out the water. Mix all the remaining ingredients.

2 Heat the oil and add the mustard seeds. When they stop sputtering, add the green chilli, stirring for $1/2$ minute and then add in the prepared papaya mixture. Mix well and remove from the fire. Serve at room temperature.

ROOTS RAITA

PREPARATION TIME: 5 MINS. • COOKING TIME: 20 MINS.

SERVES 6

Ingredients

1 cup boiled and cubed potatoes
1 cup boiled and cubed sweet potatoes
1 cup boiled and cubed yam
2 cups fresh curd, beaten
2-3 green chillies, chopped
2 tablespoons chopped coriander leaves
2 tablespoons grated coconut
Salt to taste

For tempering

2 tablespoons oil
1 teaspoon mustard seeds

Method

1 Heat the oil and add the mustard seeds. When they stop sputtering, add the green chillies; after a minute, add the potatoes, sweet potatoes and yam. Mix well and remove from the stove.

2 When the mixture cools, add the curd, salt, coriander leaves and coconut. Refrigerate till serving time.

Crisp Raw Papaya Salad–

Dalia is a roasted, puffed form of split chana dal (Bengal gram). It is readily available at Indian grocery stores.

Tondli Kachumber–

If tondli is not available, replace it with red radish or turnip.

PACHADI SALAD

PREPARATION TIME: 10 MINS. • NO COOKING

SERVES 6

Ingredients

1 cup chopped cucumber
1 apple, cubed
1 cup grapes, green or black–seeded or seedless, split into two
$^1/_4$ cup walnuts
2 cups curd
1 teaspoon cummin seeds, roasted and coarsely powdered
Apple slices, cucumber slices, and salad leaves for decoration
Salt and sugar to taste

Method

1 Drain the water from the curd. Mix the salt, sugar and powdered cummin seeds.
2 Apply a little salt to the cucumber and set aside for 15 minutes. Lightly squeeze out the water.
3 Mix the remaining ingredients with the curd. Chill before serving. Remove into a serving bowl and decorate with apple slices, cucumber slices and salad leaves.

TONDLI KACHUMBER

PREPARATION TIME: 15 MINS. • COOKING TIME: 10 MINS.

SERVES 6-8

Ingredients

$^1/_2$ cup finely chopped tondli
$^1/_2$ cup finely chopped carrot
$^1/_2$ finely chopped cucumber
$^1/_2$ grated coconut
$^1/_2$ cup chopped coriander leaves
2-3 green chillies, finely chopped
1 tablespoon lemon juice
2 tablespoons oil
Carrot and cucumber slices for decoration
A pinch of asafoetida
Salt to taste

Method

1 Heat the oil and add in the asafoetida. After a minute, add the tondli and carrot. When they change colour, remove from the stove. Cool.
2 Add the cucumber and the rest of the ingredients. Remove into a serving bowl. Decorate with sliced carrots and cucumber.

EMERALD BEAUTY SALAD

PREPARATION TIME: 15 MINS. •
COOKING TIME: 2 HOURS 5 MINS.

SERVES 10

Ingredients

- **1 packet lemon jelly crystals (85 gms.)**
- **A few drops of green colouring**
- **$^1/_4$ cup vinegar or green grape juice**
- **$^1/_2$ cup seedless green grapes, split into two**
- **$^1/_4$ cup green peas, boiled**
- **$^1/_4$ cup chopped capsicum**
- **$^1/_4$ cup chopped and boiled French beans**
- **Salad leaves, grapes, and cucumber slices for decoration**
- **$^1/_4$ teaspoon salt**

Method

1. Dissolve the lemon jelly crystals in $2^1/_4$ cups of water. Cool. Add the green grape juice, green colouring and salt. Place in the refrigerator to set. Take it out when it is semi-set. Mix in all the vegetables and grapes. Fill into a mould and chill in the refrigerator till it sets well.
2. Unmould onto a serving plate. Decorate with salad leaves, grapes and cucumber slices.

PAPAYA RAITA

PREPARATION TIME: 7 MINS. • NO COOKING

SERVES 6

Ingredients

- **1 cup thick curd**
- **1 cup mashed ripe papaya**
- **2 tablespoons honey**
- **A pinch of cinnamon**
- **$^1/_4$ teaspoon salt**

Method

Beat the curd and then add in the rest of the ingredients. Mix well and serve chilled.

FLUFFY PANEER RAITA

PREPARATION TIME: 10 MINS. • NO COOKING

SERVES 6

Ingredients

- **1 cup thick curd**
- **2 tablespoons fresh grated coconut**
- **2 tablespoons chopped coriander leaves**
- **$^1/_4$ cup paneer crumbs**
- **1 chilli, finely chopped**
- **Salt to taste**

Method

Beat the thick curd and then add in rest of the ingredients. Mix well and refrigerate till you wish to serve.

DALS & CURRIES

(a long-handled brass ladle)

Delicious vegetable preparations with gravies are called curries. Indian curries are famous all over the world. Some of the most interesting recipes are given in this chapter.

Bean and legume (dal) preparations are an excellent source of vegetable protein, vitamin B, iron, magnesium and zinc. They are also high in soluble fibres, which help lower cholesterol, stabilize blood sugar levels and reduce the occurence of certain cancers. Whenever bean preparations are served with grains like rice, wheat and vegetables, they make a complete, nourishing meal.

A variety of dals are available in India, such as gram, tur, moong, urad and lentil. Dals can be cooked separately or mixed with vegetables to create delicious recipes. People in each state of India have their own special and unique ways of cooking dals and eating them with combinations of vegetables and rice or Indian bread.

PANEER MUTTER KORMA (COTTAGE CHEESE AND GREEN PEAS CURRY)

PREPARATION TIME: 15 MINS. • COOKING TIME: 20 MINS.
SERVES 6

Ingredients

For the korma

- 3/4 cup paneer, crumbled
- 1 packet (200 gms.) tomato purée
- 1 large tomato, juice extract
- 3 tablespoons ghee
- 1 teaspoon chilli powder
- 1/4 teaspoon turmeric powder
- 1/2 teaspoon freshly roasted cummin seeds, powdered
- 1 tablespoon thick cream
- 3/4 cup green peas, boiled
- A few coriander leaves, chopped
- Salt to taste

For the masala paste

- 1/2 cup cashewnuts pieces
- 2 green chillies
- 1 tablespoon sesame seeds

Method

1 Prepare the masala paste by grinding the cashewnuts, chillies and sesame seeds with a little water.

2 Heat the ghee; add the masala paste and stir till it changes colour. Add the tomato paste and tomato juice. Mix in all the spices and simmer till the ghee separates. Add the paneer crumbs and green peas. Bring to a boil. Now add the cream and simmer for 5 minutes. Sprinkle coriander leaves on top and serve hot.

HARI DAL (GREEN DAL)

PREPARATION TIME: 10 MINS. • COOKING TIME: 30 MINS.
SERVES 6

Ingredients

- 1 cup tur dal (red gram split)
- 1 tablespoon oil
- A few curry leaves
- 2 tablespoons lemon juice
- Salt to taste

For the masala paste

- 1/2 cup grated coconut
- 2 cups coriander leaves
- 6 to 8 cloves garlic
- 4-5 green chillies
- 1/2" piece of ginger

Method

Wash the tur dal and pressure cook with 2 cups of water. Beat with an egg beater to break up all the grains. Heat the oil and add the curry leaves. After a minute, add the cooked dal and enough water to submerge the dal. Bring to a boil. Now add the salt, lemon juice and masala paste. Simmer for 8-10 minutes. Serve hot.

1 Emerald Beauty Salad p. 41

Colour photo on p. 45

1 Malijhuli Tadka Dal p. 49
2 Hari Dal p. 43

Colour photo on p. 46

RASWALI ALU KI NAV
(POTATO BOATS IN GRAVY)

PREPARATION TIME: 15 MINS. • COOKING TIME: 50 MINS.
SERVES 6

Ingredients

6 large potatoes of the same size
Oil for frying

For the stuffing

3/4 cup paneer
1/2 cup green peas, boiled
1 onion, chopped
5-6 green chillies, finely chopped
1 teaspoon ginger-garlic paste
2 tablespoons coriander leaves
1/2 cup cashewnuts, finely chopped
Salt to taste

For the tomato sauce

2 tablespoons butter
1 kg. tomatoes, extract juice
1 onion and 6 cloves garlic, made into a paste
1 tablespoon sugar
1 teaspoon red chilli powder
A pinch of garam masala
Salt to taste

For the topping

Grated cheese

Method

For the potato boats

1 Peel the potatoes and boil them partially. Cut into halves and scoop out the centres to make boats. Chop the scooped out parts of the potatoes and put aside. Fry the potato boats in oil till done.

For the stuffing

2 Heat the oil and add the onions; fry for 2 minutes. Now add the chillies and ginger-garlic paste and fry a little longer. Add the chopped potatoes and cook till done. Add the paneer, green peas, coriander leaves, cashewnut pieces and salt. Mix well and fill the potato boats with this stuffing.

For the tomato sauce

3 Melt the butter; add the onion-garlic paste and fry for a few minutes. Add the tomato juice and all the seasonings and boil till you obtain a sauce-like consistency. Pour into a baking dish. Arrange the potato boats in this. Top each boat with grated cheese and bake in the oven at 200°C for 25-30 minutes.

MALIJHULI TADKA DAL (MIXED TADKA DAL)

PREPARATION TIME: 20 MINS. • COOKING TIME: 30 MINS.

SERVES 6

Ingredients

- 1/2 cup moong dal (green gram split)
- 1/4 cup chana dal (Bengal gram split)
- 1/2 cup tur dal (red gram split)
- 1/4 cup Masoor dal (lentil)
- 1/2 teaspoon turmeric powder
- 3-4 chillies, chopped
- 1 teaspoon cummin seeds
- 1″ ginger, finely chopped
- 1 tomato, chopped
- 3-14 cloves garlic, chopped
- 3 tablespoons oil
- A few coriander leaves
- Salt to taste

Method

1 Wash all 4 dals together and soak for 15 minutes. Then pressure cook with enough water. Beat the dals with an egg beater to partially break up the grains.

2 Heat the oil and add the cummin seeds. When brown, add the dals and enough water to boil. Add turmeric powder, salt, green chillies, ginger, tomato and garlic pieces. Boil and then simmer for 10 minutes. Garnish with coriander leaves.

SUKHI CHANE KI DAL (DRY CHANA DAL)

PREPARATION TIME: 2 HOURS 5 MINS. • COOKING TIME: 30 MINS.

SERVES 6

Ingredients

- 1 cup chana dal (Bengal gram split)
- 1 teaspoon coriander powder
- 1/4 teaspoon turmeric powder
- 4-5 green chillies, split
- 1 teaspoon cummin seeds
- 2 tablespoons ghee (clarified butter)
- 2-3 red chillies, whole
- 2 Bay leaves
- 2-3 cardamoms
- 2-3 cloves
- 2 small pieces cinnamon
- 1/2″ piece of ginger, minced
- 1 tablespoon sugar (optional)
- 3 tablespoons grated coconut
- A few coriander leaves, chopped
- Salt to taste

Method

Wash the split chana dal and soak for 2 hours. Pressure cook with a little salt. Do not add too much water. Heat the ghee and add the red chillies, cummin seeds, Bay leaves, cardamom, cinnamon and cloves. When they turn brown, add the green chillies, ginger, coconut, turmeric and coriander powder. Roast for a minute and then add the cooked dal.

1 Raswali Alu Ki Nav p. 44

Colour photo on p. 47

---

1 Masala Chawal Ke Parathe p. 54
2 Gajar Ke Parathe p. 56
3 Palak Ki Puri p. 55
4 Do Rangi Puri p. 54

Colour photo on p. 48

Kathal Rimzim Curry–

This curry can be made with mixed vegetables instead of Jackfruit pieces.

Mix well and add salt. Add the sugar if you wish. Cook the dal with the masala for a few minutes for the flavour to set in. Allow excess water to evaporate by boiling and making it dry. Sprinkle the coriander leaves and serve hot or cold.

KATHAL RIMZIM CURRY
(JACKFRUIT CURRY)

PREPARATION TIME: 20 MINS. • COOKING TIME: 45 MINS.
SERVES 6

Ingredients

2½ cups raw, tender Jackfruit pieces
½ cup green peas, boiled
¼ cup oil
½ teaspoon turmeric powder
2 teaspoons red chilli powder
A few coriander leaves, chopped
Salt to taste

For the masala paste

2 large onions, sliced
6 green chillies, chopped
1″ piece of ginger, chopped
1 teaspoon cummin seeds
1 cup grated coconut
3-4 cloves
3-4 cinnamon
6-8 black peppercorns
2 tablespoons oil
2 large tomatoes, chopped (or extract juice)

Method

1 Cook the Jackfruit pieces in 1 cup water with a little salt, in the pressure cooker.
2 To prepare the masala paste, heat 2 tablespoons of oil and add the cummin seeds, cloves, cinnamon and black pepper; sauté for a minute. Now add the onions and sauté till the onions turn soft and pink. Add the green chillies and ginger; sauté for 1 more minute. Then add the coconut and heat through. Remove from heat. Cool and make into a paste.
3 Heat ¼ cup oil. Add the masala paste and sauté till the oil separates. Add the tomato juice, turmeric and red chilli powder; sauté till the oil separates. Add the Jackfruit pieces with water, mix well and cook till the gravy turns thick. Now add salt to taste and put in the green peas. Serve hot with coriander sprinkled on top.

BHUTTE KI KOFTA CURRY
(CORN BALL CURRY)

PREPARATION TIME: 15 MINS. • COOKING TIME: 30 MINS.
SERVES 6

Ingredients

For the kofta

- 1 cup fresh corn, grated
- 1/4 cup flattened rice
- 1 potato, boiled and mashed
- 2 tablespoons lemon juice
- 3 green chillies, finely chopped
- 1/4 teaspoon turmeric powder
- 2 tablespoons corn flour
- Oil for deep frying
- Salt and sugar to taste

For the gravy

- 3 tablespoons butter
- 1 large onion, chopped
- 3 green chillies, chopped
- 1 tablespoon flour
- 1 cup milk
- 1/4 cup tomato ketchup
- 2 tablespoons fresh cream
- 1 teaspoon red chilli powder
- A few coriander leaves, chopped
- Salt to taste

Method

For the koftas

1 To prepare the koftas, wash the flattened rice and mix the rest of the ingredients for the koftas.

2 Mix well and make into small balls. Deep fry the balls in oil till a golden-brown.

For the gravy

3 Heat the butter; add the green chillies and onions and sauté till they turn soft. Add the flour and sauté for another minute. Add the milk and mix well, stirring continuously till thick. Add the tomato ketchup, salt, red chilli powder and fresh cream. Add water to adjust the consistency of the gravy and then bring to a boil.

4 Add the koftas just before serving. Sprinkle chopped coriander leaves over the top of the curry.

KAJU ANGOORI CURRY
(CASHEW AND GRAPE CURRY)

PREPARATION TIME: 15 MINS. • COOKING TIME: 25 MINS.
SERVES 4-6

Ingredients

- 4 tablespoons oil
- 1 cup seedless green grapes
- 1/2 cup pieces of cashewnuts
- 5 tablespoons tomato sauce
- 1 tablespoon green chilli-garlic sauce
- 1/2 teaspoon red chilli powder
- A pinch of black pepper powder
- A few coriander leaves, chopped
- Salt to taste

For the masala paste

- 1/2 cup chopped onions
- 1 big tomato
- 3-4 cloves garlic

Kaju Angoori Curry –

In place of green grapes, a mixture of different varieties of grapes can be used in the curry.

1 tablespoon sugar
2-3 pieces cinnamon
2-3 cloves
1/2" piece of ginger
2-3 green chillies
1/4 cup cashewnut pieces

Method

1. Heat the oil and fry the masala paste in it till the oil separates.
2. Add the tomato sauce, chilli-garlic sauce, sugar, red chilli powder, cinnamon, cloves, black pepper and salt. Mix well and fry for 5 minutes.
3. Add the cashewnut pieces and 1/2 cup water, simmering for a few minutes.
4. Now add the grapes. Keep gravy covered for a few minutes for the flavour to set in. Sprinkle coriander leaves on top and serve hot.

MASALA SPROUTED MOONG (SPICY SPROUTED GREEN GRAM)

PREPARATION TIME: SPROUTING TIME: 5 MINS.
COOKING TIME: 20 MINS.
SERVES 4-6

Ingredients

1 1/2 cups sprouted moong (green gram)
1 cup grated coconut
1/4 cup coriander leaves
2 green chillies, finely chopped
2 tablespoons lemon juice
Salt to taste

For tempering

2 tablespoons oil
1 teaspoon mustard seeds
2-3 red dry chillies
A pinch of asafoetida

Method

1 Take the well-sprouted moong in a vessel. Add enough water to cover and add 1/4 teaspoon salt. Bring to a boil. Drain off the water and remove skins from the moong as far as possible.
2 Mix the skinned moong with the coconut, coriander leaves, green chillies, lemon juice and salt.
3 Prepare tempering by first heating the oil. Add the mustard seeds. When they stop sputtering, add the dry red chillies and asafoetida. After 1/2 minute, pour tempering over the prepared moong. Mix well. Serve at room temperature.

With a little bit of imagination and innovation, one can create numerous kinds of parathas and puris, which are tasty, wholesome and nutritious. By using seasonal vegetables, different spices, a variety of dals and flours, one can invent wonderful new recipes for puris, parathas and breads. Make use of leftover food like cooked rice, dry dals, boiled potatoes or yam. Serve either hot or cold with curries, pickles or even with chutnies.

PURIS, PARATHAS & INDIAN BREADS

(an elaborately fashioned brass oven)

Do Rangi Puri–

Tri-coloured puris can be made by adding green spinach puri dough to the dough already mentioned.

DO RANGI PURI (TWO-COLOUR PURIS)

PREPARATION TIME: 20 MINS. • COOKING TIME: 25 MINS.
MAKES 25 PURIS

Ingredients

For the red portion
1 cup flour
1/4 cup grated beetroot
1 teaspoon red chilli powder
1 1/2 tablespoons oil
Salt to taste

For the white portion
1 cup flour
1 tablespoon curd
1 tablespoon dessicated coconut
1 1/2 tablespoons oil
Oil for deep frying
Salt to taste

Method

1 For the red portion, make a purée of the beetroot, red chilli powder and salt, in the blender; add this to the flour. Also add 1 1/2 tablespoons oil. Mix well and make a stiff dough using just enough water; knead well with a little oil. Divide the dough into 25 balls.

2 For the white portion, mix all the ingredients with the flour, making a stiff dough using just enough water. Knead well with a little oil. Divide the dough into 25 balls.

3 Now take one red and one white ball and mix them together. Press and roll out the puri. Similarly, make all the puris. Deep fry in oil and serve hot.

MASALA CHAWAL KE PARATHE (SPICY RICE PARATHAS)

PREPARATION TIME: 10 MINS. • COOKING TIME: 25 MINS.
MAKES 10 PARATHAS

Ingredients

1 cup flour
1 cup wheat flour
1/2 cup cooked rice
1/4 cup coriander leaves
1 teaspoon red chilli powder
1 teaspoon ginger-green chilli paste
1/4 teaspoon turmeric powder
2 tablespoons curd
2 tablespoons oil
A pinch of asafoetida
Oil for shallow frying
Salt to taste

Method

1 Mash the rice slightly. Add the rice to the flour, along with all the spices and coriander leaves; mix well. Prepare a stiff dough by adding a little water. Make 10 balls.

2 Roll out each ball with a little dry flour to 4″ diameter circles. Shallow fry in oil. Serve hot or cold.

SHAKKARAND KI PURI
(SWEET POTATO PURIS)

PREPARATION TIME: 10 MINS. • COOKING TIME: 25 MINS.
MAKES 20-25 PURIS

Ingredients

2 cups flour
1/2 cup boiled and mashed sweet potato
1/4 cup powdered sugar
1/2 teaspoon cardamom powder
A pinch of soda bicarbonate
3 tablespoons melted ghee
1 teaspoon sesame seeds (til)
Milk as required for making the dough
Oil for deep frying

Method

1 Mix all the ingredients with the flour, adding milk carefully to make a stiff dough; knead well with a little ghee. Divide the dough into 20-25 balls and roll out each ball into a small circle with a little dry flour.
2 Deep fry in oil and serve hot.

PALAK KI PURI
(SPINACH PURIS)

PREPARATION TIME: 10 MINS. • COOKING TIME: 25 MINS.
MAKES 20-25 PURIS

Ingredients

1 cup wheat flour
1 cup flour
1/2 cup spinach paste
1 teaspoon ginger-green chilli paste
6 cloves garlic, minced
A pinch of soda bicarbonate
3 tablespoons oil
Oil for deep frying
Salt to taste

Method

1 Combine both varieties of flour in a deep dish. Add the spinach paste, ginger-green chilli paste, minced garlic, soda bicarbonate, salt and 3 tablespoons of oil. Mix well, adding water carefully to make a stiff dough. Knead well with a little oil. Divide the dough into 20-25 balls and roll out into small circles with dry flour.
2 Deep fry in oil and serve hot.

Gajar Ke Parathe–

The carrot stuffing can be replaced with raw papaya stuffing.

Hare Matar Bhare Pude

Pudas are made just like pancakes. They can be plain or stuffed.

GAJAR KE PARATHE (STUFFED CARROT PARATHAS)

PREPARATION TIME: 10 MINS. • COOKING TIME: 35 MINS.

MAKES 10 PIECES

Ingredients

2 cups grated carrot
2 cups flour
2 tablespoons gram flour
1/2 teaspoon cummin seeds
1/4 teaspoon asafoetida
2 teaspoons red chilli powder
4 tablespoons oil
Oil for shallow frying
Salt to taste

Method

1 Lightly squeeze the grated carrots and put the squeezed out juice aside. Heat 2 tablespoons oil; add the cummin seeds and stir till brown. Add the asafoetida and grated carrot, cooking them for 3-4 minutes. Now mix in the gram flour, salt and red chilli powder. Roast the mixture on low heat till it becomes dry. Remove from the stove and cool. Divide into 10 parts.

2 To the flour, add 2 tablespoons oil, salt and the carrot juice; mix thoroughly. Add just enough water to make a stiff dough and knead with a little oil. Divide the dough into 10 balls. Roll each ball into a small round. Put in one portion of carrot stuffing and seal all sides. Roll out again carefully to make a stuffed paratha. Shallow fry with oil. Serve hot.

HARE MATAR BHARE PUDE (GREEN PEAS PANCAKES)

PREPARATION TIME: 20 MINS. • COOKING TIME: 30 MINS.

MAKES 12-15 PUDAS

Ingredients

1 cup green peas, crushed
1/2 cup rice flour
1/2 cup gram flour
1 1/2 tablespoons ginger-green chilli paste
1/4 teaspoon turmeric powder
Oil for shallow frying
Salt to taste

For the stuffing

1 cup boiled and mashed potatoes,
1/2 cup paneer
3 tablespoons oil
1 tomato, chopped
1 onion, chopped
1 teaspoon cummin seeds
1/4 cup chopped coriander leaves
1/4 cup grated coconut
1 tablespoon amchoor (dry mango powder)
1 tablespoon ginger-green chilli paste
1/4 teaspoon turmeric powder
1/4 teaspoon garam masala
Salt to taste

Method

For the pudas (pancakes)

1 Mix all the ingredients and add water to make a loose pancake batter.

For the stuffing

1 Heat the oil and add the cummin seeds. After a minute, add the onions and sauté till they turn light pink. Add the tomatoes and all the remaining spices and keep on stirring till the oil separates.
2 Add in the paneer, potatoes, coriander and coconut. Mix well and remove from the stove.
3 Make small pancakes with a little oil. Put stuffing on one side and fold over the pancake into half. Lightly press and cook on both sides till crisp. Serve hot with tomato ketchup or Green Coriander Chutney (refer to chapter on Pickles, Chutnies & Masalas).

BAJRA PUDE
(MILLET PANCAKES)

PREPARATION TIME: 45 MINS. • COOKING TIME: 30 MINS.

MAKES 10 PUDAS

Ingredients

1 cup bajra flour (millet flour)
1/2 cup gram flour or rice flour
1/2 cup sprouted moong
1/4 cup grated onion
1 tablespoon green garlic with leaves, chopped; or 2-3 cloves garlic, minced
1/2 cup curd
1/4 cup chopped coriander leaves
1 tablespoon ginger-green chilli paste
2 tablespoons oil
Oil for shallow frying
Salt to taste

Method

1 Put all the ingredients for the pudas into a vessel. Mix well and add just enough water to make a loose batter. Set aside for at least 1/2 hour.
2 Make round pudas on a skillet. Apply a little oil onto both sides and shallow fry till done. Serve hot with Green Tomato Chutney (refer to chapter on Pickles, Chutnies & Masalas).

Masala Panki –

If banana leaves are not available, make the pankis on a non-stick skillet.

MITHI MAWA ROTI
(SWEET MAWA BREAD)

PREPARATION TIME: 3 HOURS 15 MINS.
COOKING TIME: 30 MINS.
MAKES 10 ROTIS

Ingredients

2 cups flour
1/2 cup curd
1 tablespoon powdered sugar
3 tablespoons melted ghee
1 teaspoon sesame seeds (til)
1/4 teaspoon salt
Ghee for glazing

For the topping

A few very thin slices of almonds and pistachios

For the stuffing

2 tablespoons powdered sugar
10 tablespoons of mawa (khoya)

Method

1 Take all the ingredients for the dough and mix well. Add just enough water to make a soft dough and knead well with ghee. Cover and set aside for 2-3 hours. Knead again and make 10 balls.

2 Roll out a roti with a little dry flour, to a 2″ diameter round. Stuff 1 tablespoon of the sugar and mawa mixture into it. Seal all sides and make a ball again. Roll out to a 5″ diameter.

3 Roast on a skillet until it turns a light brown colour on both sides.

4 Apply ghee as glaze and sprinkle a few almond and pistachios slices. Make all the rotis in the same way. Serve hot.

MASALA PANKI
(SPICY THICK PANCAKES)

PREPARATION TIME: 3 HOURS 10 MINS.
COOKING TIME: 50 MINS.
MAKES 6-7 PANKIS

Ingredients

2 cups rice flour
1 cup curd
1/2 teaspoon turmeric powder
1 teaspoon cummin seeds
1 teaspoon ginger-green chilli paste
1/2 cup finely chopped methi (fenugreek leaves)
1 teaspoon sugar
1 onion, grated
1/4 cup grated coconut
3 tablespoons ghee, melted
6-7 pairs of banana leaves, 6″ × 8″ size
Oil for glazing
Salt to taste

Method

1 Place all the ingredients in a deep vessel. Mix well and then add just enough water to make a soft dough which can be spread easily but does not run. Cover and set aside the dough aside for at least 2-4 hours.

2 Take the cleaned banana leaves and apply oil on the right side of the leaves. Spread the prepared panki dough on one leaf, with a spoon, to an oval shape of about 5″ long and 4″ wide and $^1/_2$″ thick. Cover with another leaf. Place on a hot skillet and cover with a lid. Cook on medium heat. Turn sides after a few minutes and cook till pink spots appear on both sides. To check if the panki is done, open the banana leaf gently. Remove the leaves and serve hot with a pickle.

MASALEWALI BHUTTE KI ROTI (SPICY CORN BREAD)

PREPARATION TIME: 1 HOUR 15 MINS.
COOKING TIME: 30 MINS.
MAKES 12 ROTIS

Ingredients

1 cup maize (corn) flour
$^1/_2$ cup flour
$^1/_2$ cup wheat flour
$^1/_2$ cup curd
$^1/_4$ cup coriander leaves
$^1/_2$ teaspoon turmeric powder
1$^1/_2$ teaspoons ajwain
1 teaspoon ginger-green chilli paste
3 tablespoons oil
Salt to taste
Ghee for glazing
Warm water to bind the dough

Method

1 Take all the ingredients for the dough and mix well. Add warm water and make a soft dough. Knead well with a little extra oil. Put the dough in a vessel, cover and set aside for an hour.
2 Knead the dough again and make 12 balls. Roll out each ball to a 6″ diameter using a little dry flour.
3 Dry roast both sides on a griddle till the roti has light pink spots.
4 Glaze the roti with a little ghee and serve hot.
5 Make all the rotis in the same way.

PULLAOS

(a large copper cooking pot used for making dals, lentils and rice dishes)

Indian cuisine is a rich source of traditional as well as delightfully innovative rice recipes. Being the staple food for many people, rice preparations are filling yet easy to digest. There is nothing more satisfying than a steaming bowl of rice with dal or rasam and some tongue-tickling pickle.

Here are a few recipes combining rice and various nutritious ingredients, including sprouted moong, spinach and other vegetables.

KHICHDA
(DAL AND RICE)

PREPARATION TIME: OVERNIGHT & 10 MINS.
COOKING TIME: 45 MINS.
SERVES 8-10

Ingredients

2 cups broken wheat (from the market)
2 tablespoons tur dal (red gram split)
2 tablespoons chana dal (Bengal gram split)
1/2 cup rice
3 potatoes boiled and cut into big pieces
1″ piece of ginger, minced
3 chillies, minced
1 tablespoon caraway seeds (shahjeeru)
5-6 cloves garlic, minced
1 teaspoon cummin seeds
1/2 cup ghee
Salt to taste

To garnish

Mint leaves
Fried onions
Lemon slices
Garam masala (readymade)

Method

1 Wash the broken wheat and submerge in water and soak overnight. Next day, in the same water, add the rice, dals, 1/2 the ginger, the chillies, caraway seeds and salt. Mix well and pressure cook. Remove from the cooker and mash.

2 Heat the ghee and brown the garlic and cummin seeds. Add the wheat mixture. Mix thoroughly and heat for a few minutes.

3 Heat a little more ghee and sauté the remaining spices. Add the potato pieces and salt; mix well. Add this to the wheat mixture. Remove into a serving bowl. Decorate with mint leaves, fried onions, garam masala and lemon slices.

HARIALI PULLAO
(GREEN PULLAO)

PREPARATION TIME: 15 MINS. • COOKING TIME: 40 MINS.
SERVES 6-8

Ingredients

2 cups Basmati rice
1 cup green tur or green chana or fresh double beans
1/4 cup ghee
2-3 cloves
2-3 cinnamon pieces
Salt to taste

For the masala paste

3/4 cup coriander leaves
3/4 cup spinach leaves
2-3 green chillies
1/2″ piece of ginger
2-3 cloves garlic

Method

1 Wash and soak the rice for 15 minutes.

2 Heat the ghee and brown the cinnamon and cloves for 1/2 minute. Sauté the green masala paste till the ghee separates.

3 Now add the rice and the green tur, stirring for 5 minutes. Add salt and just enough hot water to cook the rice. Bring to a boil. Reduce heat to simmer, cover and cook till done.

MANPASAND PULLAO

PREPARATION TIME: 15 MINS. • COOKING TIME: 50 MINS.
SERVES 6-8

Ingredients

2 cups Basmati rice
2 cups sliced onions
1/4 cup sprouted moong (green gram)
1/4 cup sprouted chana (Bengal gram)
1/4 cup sprouted muth (muth beans)
1/4 cup sprouted peas
1 cup coconut milk
1/2 cup ghee
8 cloves garlic, minced
1″ ginger, minced
1-2 green chillies, minced
8-10 cloves
6-8 pieces cinnamon
6-8 cardamoms
10 peppercorns
2 Bay leaves
2 tablespoons lemon juice
Salt to taste

Method

1 Wash the rice and soak for 15 minutes.
2 In a pan, melt the ghee and fry the onion slices till they turn a golden brown. Set aside 1/2 the onions. Sauté the cloves, cinnamon, cardamom, peppercorns and Bay leaves along with the remaining onions, for a minute. Add all the sprouted pulses and mix well. Add 1/2 of the minced ginger, garlic, chillies, and salt and sauté for a few minutes. Then add the coconut milk, cover and cook for 10 minutes.
3 Now add the soaked rice, along with the remaining minced ginger, garlic, chillies and salt. Mix everything well and add enough hot water to cook the rice. Cover and pressure cook till done.

MOONG PULLAO
(GREEN GRAM PULLAO)

PREPARATION TIME: 15 MINS. • COOKING TIME: 30 MINS.
SERVES 6-8

Ingredients

For the rice

1½ cups rice
1 cup sprouted moong (green gram)
2 tablespoons ghee
2-3 cloves
2-3 cinnamon pieces
2-3 cardamoms
Salt to taste

For the masala paste

1 cup coriander leaves
½ cup mint leaves
3-4 green chillies
½″ piece of ginger
¼ cup grated coconut
1 tablespoon lemon juice

For the curd layer

2½ cups curd
2 teaspoons red chilli powder
Salt to taste

Method

1 Drain the water from the curd by tying it in a muslin cloth. Mix in the salt and chilli powder. Set aside in the refrigerator.
2 Wash the rice and soak for 10 minutes.
3 Heat the ghee and add the cloves, cinnamon and cardamom. After a minute add the sprouted moong and sauté for about 2 minutes. Add the rice, salt and enough hot water to cook the rice. Cover and let it simmer.
4 When the rice is almost done, mix in the ground masala paste. Cover again and cook for another 10 minutes for the flavour to set in.
5 Take a ring mould of 8″ diameter and grease it with oil. Spread half of the rice in the mould and press firmly; put in a layer of curd and cover with the remaining rice. Compress to acquire the shape of the mould. Invert onto a serving plate or dish.

BUTTA AUR DHINGRI PULLAO
(CORN & MUSHROOM PULLAO)

PREPARATION TIME: 10 MINS. • COOKING TIME: 30 MINS.
SERVES 6-8

Ingredients

2 cups rice
1 onion, chopped
1 capsicum, chopped
1 cup mushroom pieces
1 cup corn, boiled
4 tablespoons ghee
2 tablespoons Biryani masala (readymade)
¼ teaspoon turmeric powder
Salt to taste

1 Gatte Ke Chawal p. 64
2 Moong Pullao p. 63

Colour photo on p. 65

---

1 Doodhi Muthia p. 72
2 Sabzi Muthia p. 73

Colour photo on p. 66

Method

1 Cook rice in salt water till done but retains firm grains.
2 Heat the ghee and add the onions and sauté for a few minutes. Add the capsicum and mushroom pieces and stir. Then add in the corn, Biryani masala, turmeric powder and salt; stir for another minute. Add the cooked rice, mix well and serve hot.

GATTE KE CHAWAL
(RICE WITH DUMPLINGS)

PREPARATION TIME: 20 MINS. • COOKING TIME: 50 MINS.

SERVES 6-8

Ingredients

For Gatte

1¹/₄ cups gram flour
2 teaspoons red chilli powder
2 teaspoons cummin and coriander seed powder
¹/₄ teaspoon turmeric powder
¹/₂ teaspoon ajwain
1 tablespoon oil
A pinch of asafoetida
Salt to taste

For the rice

2 cups rice
¹/₄ cup chopped and boiled French beans
¹/₄ cup chopped and boiled carrot
¹/₂ teaspoon cummin seeds
¹/₄ teaspoon turmeric powder
3 tablespoons oil
Salt to taste

Method

1 Take all the ingredients for the Gatte in a plate and mix well. Add a little water to make a puri-like dough. Divide it into 6 balls and roll out each ball into long rolls of a finger thickness.
2 Take water in a broad vessel and boil. Put the rolls carefully into the boiling water. They will sink to the bottom. Cover the vessel, allowing the Gatte to simmer for 15 minutes till they cook and turn a pale colour. They will float to the surface. Remove with a strainer and cool. Cut into small pieces of ¹/₂″ size.
3 Heat the oil and sauté the cummin seeds for a minute. Add the washed rice, salt and turmeric powder and stir for a minute. Add enough hot water to cook the rice. Cover till almost done. Mix in the French beans, carrot and the Gatte pieces. Serve hot.

DALCHAWAL PALIDU
(LENTIL – RICE PALIDU)

PREPARATION TIME: 10 MINS. • COOKING TIME: 1 HOUR
SERVES 8-10

Ingredients

For the Dalchawal

1 cup tur dal (red gram split)
2 cups rice
½ cup oil
4-5 cloves
1-2 sticks cinnamon
1 teaspoon cummin seeds
8-10 cloves garlic, minced
½ teaspoon turmeric powder
Salt to taste

For the Palidu

3 cups dal water
½ cup rice water
1 tablespoon oil
1 teaspoon cummin seeds
½ teaspoon fenugreek (methi) seeds
5-6 cloves garlic, minced
2 tablespoons gram flour
1 teaspoon red chilli powder
5-6 cloves garlic, minced
2 teaspoons coriander-cummin powder
4-5 pieces cocum or 1 tablespoon lemon juice
Salt to taste

Method

For the Dalchawal

1 Cook the dal with a lot of water, adding salt and turmeric powder. Remove from heat and allow to settle before draining off the water. Set aside for the palidu.
2 Cook the rice with water and salt; when done, drain off the extra water and retain for the palidu.
3 Heat the oil and stir in the cummin seeds and sauté till they turn brown. Add the garlic, cinnamon, cloves and sauté for a minute. Then add the cooked dal, rice, turmeric powder and salt. Mix well and allow it to simmer on a low flame till it turns thick.

For the Palidu

1 Heat oil and brown the cummin seeds; then add the fenugreek, garlic, gram flour, chilli powder and coriander-cummin powder. Stir well. Add the dal rice water and salt and let it boil. Add the drumstick pieces and cook till the sticks become soft; add the cocum and boil for a little longer. Serve with the Dalchawal.

1 **Bhakarwadi** p. 76
2. **Suji Ghughara** p. 89
3 **Kesar Malai Peda** p. 95
4 **Goba Puri** p. 76

Colour photo on p. 67

1 **Chawal Ki Chakri** p. 75
2. **Ajwain Puri** p. 74
3. **Mithe Shakkarpara** p. 75
4. **Masala Chivda** p. 74

Colour photo on p. 68

SIMLA MIRCH PULLAO (CAPSICUM PULLAO)

PREPARATION TIME: 20 MINS. • COOKING TIME: 35 MINS.
SERVES 6-8

Ingredients

For the Pullao

1/4 cup ghee
2 cardamoms
2 cloves
1 stick cinnamom
1 1/2 cups long grained rice
1 cup cabbage pieces
2 potatoes, cut into big pieces
2 capsicums, cut into big pieces
1/2 cup green peas
2 big onions, chopped
3 cloves garlic, chopped
1/4 cup pieces of apricot or prunes
1/4 cup cashewnut pieces, fried
2 onions, sliced and fried separately
Salt to taste

For the Masala Paste

2 tablespoons coriander seeds
1 cup coriander leaves
1/2″ piece of ginger
3-4 green chillies

For the Tikkha Dahi

2 cups curd
2 tablespoons finely chopped coriander leaves
2 green chillies, finely chopped
2 teaspoon cummin seeds, roasted and powdered
Salt to taste

Method

For the Pullao

1. Fry the cardamom, cinnamon and cloves in the ghee for 2 minutes.
2. Add the washed rice, ground masala paste, vegetables, onion pieces, garlic, apricot pieces and salt. Sauté the mixture for a few minutes, adding just enough warm water to cook the ingredients. Cover the pan and cook on medium heat till almost done.
3. Then mix in the cashewnut pieces and fried onions and cook for a few more minutes. Serve hot with Tikkha Dahi.

For the Tikkha Dahi

1. Beat the curd to a creamy consistency; add the other ingredients.
2. Keep cool till time to serve.

SAVOURIES

This chapter brings to you a variety of delicious savoury dishes. Some are dry and crispy snacks like Masala Chivda, Ajwain Puris and Rice Chakris. These savouries can be prepared in advance and preserved for a few days. They are handy tea-time snacks for children, who are hungry all the time. Some of these delicious preparations like Gobapuris, Bhakarwadi and Chakris, are made at festival time in India, especially during Dipavali.

Some savouries like Curd Samosas and Chatpat Sev, do very well for a tea party menu. Kalmi Bade and Muthias are traditional dishes that can be served as side dishes or as a snack. Muthias have an excellent combination of various flours, spices and vegetables, including the leafy ones. They are steamed in a special steam cooker and are easy to prepare and are extremely nourishing.

(a decorated copper coffee pot)

...thia –

...uthia can be ... a similar mu..ner. Use 1 cup grated white radish and 1 cup chopped green leaves of radish, instead of white pumpkin. The rest of the ingredients, such as the flours and spices, and the method of preparation, are the same as for the Doodhi Muthia.

DOODHI MUTHIA
(WHITE PUMPKIN STEAMED ROLLS)

PREPARATION TIME: 15 MINS. • COOKING TIME: 50 MINS.
SERVES 6-8

Ingredients

1½ cups grated white pumpkin
¾ cup coarse wheat flour (like semolina)
½ cup wheat flour
¼ cup gram flour
1 teaspoon turmeric powder
2 teaspoons sugar
¼ teaspoon soda bicarbonate
¼ teaspoon asafoetida
2 teaspoons red chilli powder
2 teaspoons cummin-coriander seed powder
1 teaspoon ginger-green chilli paste
3-4 tablespoons oil
¼ cup chopped coriander leaves
¼ cup grated coconut
Curd as required
Salt to taste

For tempering

3-4 tablespoons oil
2 teaspoons mustard seeds

Method

1 Fill the steam cooker with water to half its capacity. Put on the stove to heat.

2 Take all the flours in a thali. Mix all the spices, the oil and add the grated pumpkin with its water. Mix well but lightly, keeping the mixture loose. Add the curd as required. Make big oblongs with oily hands and arrange them in an oiled plate of the steam cooker. Close the cooker and pressure cook on a medium flame for 25-30 minutes. Do not open the lid for another 10 minutes. Then take the plate out and cool for 15 minutes. Cut slices and serve with a little oil poured over them. Serve freshly-made Muthias with Green Coriander Chutney or any pickle (refer to chapter on Pickles, Chutnies & Masalas).

3 Muthias can also be served in another way. Heat the oil and add mustard seeds. When they stop sputtering, add the sliced Muthias and mix thoroughly. Sprinkle chopped coriander leaves and grated coconut before serving hot.

SABZI MUTHIA
(STEAMED VEGETABLE BALLS)

PREPARATION TIME: 15 MINS. • COOKING TIME: 50 MINS.

SERVES 6-8

Ingredients

- 1 cup chopped fenugreek leaves (methi)
- 1 cup chopped spinach leaves (palak bhaji)
- 1/2 cup chopped lettuce leaves
- 1/2 cup chopped spring onions with tender leaves or 1 onion, grated
- 4-5 cloves garlic, crushed
- 3/4 cup coarse wheat flour (like semolina)
- 1/2 cup wheat flour
- 1/4 cup gram flour
- 1 teaspoon turmeric powder
- 2 teaspoons sugar
- 1/4 teaspoon soda bicarbonate
- 1/4 teaspoon asafoetida
- 2 teaspoons red chilli powder
- 2 teaspoons cummin-coriander seed powder
- 1 teaspoon ginger-green chilli paste
- 3-4 tablespoons oil
- 1/4 cup chopped coriander leaves
- 1/4 cup grated coconut
- Curd as required
- Salt to taste

For tempering

- 3-4 tablespoons oil
- 2 teaspoons mustard seeds

Method

1 Take all the leafy vegetables in a thali; add salt and sugar and rub with your hands till the vegetables become soft and watery.

2 Then add all the spices and flours. Mix well but lightly, keeping the mixture loose. Add the curd as required. Make large oblongs with oily hands and arrange them in an oiled plate of the steam cooker. Close the cooker and cook on a medium flame for 25-30 minutes. Do not open the lid for another 10 minutes. Then take the plate out and cool for 15 minutes. Cut slices and serve with a little oil poured over them. Serve freshly made Muthias with Green Coriander Chutney or with any pickle (refer to chapter on Pickles, Chutnies & Masalas).

3 Muthias can also be served in another way. Heat the oil and add mustard seeds. When they stop sputtering, add the sliced Muthias, mixing thoroughly. Sprinkle chopped coriander leaves and grated coconut before serving hot.

Masala Chivda –

Cashewnuts, almonds and kishmis (raisins) can be fried and added to the chivda.

Ajwain Puri –

This is a dry teatime snack, which can be preserved for a few days. It tastes great with any pickle.

MASALA CHIVDA
(SPICY CRISP SNACK)

PREPARATION TIME: 10 MINS. • COOKING TIME: 30 MINS.

MAKES 3 CUPS

Ingredients

2 cups thick flattened rice (poha)
1/2 cup peanuts
1/4 cup dalia (roasted gram dal)
3-4 green chillies, cut into long pieces
1/4 teaspoon turmeric powder
1 teaspoon red chilli powder
A few slices dry coconut
A few curry leaves
A big pinch of citric acid, powdered
Oil for frying
Salt and powdered sugar to taste

Method

1 Heat oil and deep fry the poha. Remove onto an absorbent piece of paper to draw out the excess oil.

2 Heat oil in a pan, add the peanuts and dalia and sauté till they turn a light pink colour; add to the fried poha.

3 Heat a little oil and first sauté the green chillies and then the curry leaves, until crisp; add to the fried poha.

4 Taking a little more oil, sauté the coconut slices until they turn light brown and add to the fried poha. Now add all the spices such as salt, powdered sugar, citric acid, turmeric powder and red chilli powder and mix well with the poha. Store in a bottle and use as a tea-time snack.

AJWAIN PURI
(CAROM SEED PURIS)

PREPARATION TIME: 10 MINS. • COOKING TIME: 20 MINS.

MAKES 25 PURIS

Ingredients

1 cup flour
1 cup semolina flour
2 teaspoons ajwain
1/4 teaspoon turmeric powder
1/4 cup melted ghee
Oil for frying
Salt to taste

Method

1 Take both varieties of flour and add them to the ajwain, turmeric powder, salt and melted ghee. Mix well. Make a tight dough with water. Set aside for at least 15 minutes. Knead well with oil.

2 Make tiny balls and roll out thick, round puris. Deep fry in oil till they turn light pink in colour. Each puri will rise and become crisp.

MITHE SHAKKARPARA
(SWEET CRISPY SNACK)

PREPARATION TIME: 10 MINS. • COOKING TIME: 30 MINS.

MAKES MANY PIECES

Ingredients

2 cups flour
½ cup milk
½ cup sugar
4 tablespoons ghee
2 tablespoons sesame seeds
Oil or ghee for deep frying
½ teaspoon salt

Method

1 Dissolve the ghee and sugar in warm milk. Use this mixture to make a tight dough with the flour. Add the sesame seeds. Knead well and prepare large balls.

2 Roll out thick. Cut into small diamond-shaped pieces. Deep fry till pinkish in colour and crisp. Remove the deep fried shakkarparas onto an absorbent piece of paper to remove the excess oil. They can then be stored for a few days and will remain crisp.

CHAWAL KI CHAKRI
(RICE WHEELS)

PREPARATION TIME: 10 MINS. • COOKING TIME: 30 MINS.

MAKES 24 PIECES

Ingredients

2 cups rice flour
½ cup curd
¼ teaspoon turmeric powder
4 tablespoons thick cream
2 tablespoons sesame seeds
1 teaspoon cummin seeds
1 teaspoon ginger-green chilli paste
1 teaspoon red chilli powder
Oil for deep frying
Salt to taste

Method

1 Place all the ingredients and the rice flour in a vessel. Mix well and add enough water to obtain a piping consistency. Fill this dough in a chakri machine and prepare spiral circles on a piece of paper.

2 Drop the chakri pieces into the heated oil and deep fry till golden brown. The chakris should remain crisp even after cooling.

Chawal Ki Chakri–

The wheels machine is like a cookie-press, where a disk with a star-shaped hole is fitted. If these two machines are not available, fill mixture in a piping bag (like the one used for frosting cakes) fitted with a star nozzle and use this to make the chakris.

GOBA PURI
(STUFFED PURIS)

PREPARATION TIME: 20 MINS. • COOKING TIME: 30 MINS.
MAKES 20 PURIES

Ingredients

For the white dough
- 1 1/2 cups flour
- 1/4 cup melted ghee
- 1/2 teaspoon salt
- 1/2 teaspoon cummin seeds, roasted and powdered
- 2 tablespoons melted ghee

For the yellow dough
- 3/4 cup gram flour
- 1/4 teaspoon black pepper, coarsely powdered
- Ghee for deep frying
- 1/4 teaspoon salt

Method

1 Separately prepare puri-like dough for the white and yellow portions. Knead well and make an equal number of balls from each.

2 Roll out a white ball into a small round. Put a yellow ball in the center and cover it. Roll out again to make a small round. Make small holes with a fork all over it. Deep fry till it turns light pink and crisp.

BHAKARVADI
(FANCY SPICY ROLLS)

PREPARATION TIME: 15 MINS. • COOKING TIME: 1 HOUR
MAKES 30-35 PIECES

Ingredients

For the masala paste
- 3-4 Kashmiri chillies
- 4-5 Bay leaves
- 5 cloves
- 1″ cinnamon piece
- 1/4 cup coriander seeds
- 10 peppercorns
- 1 teaspoon oil

For the filling
- 1 1/2 cups dry grated coconut
- 1/4 cup sesame seeds
- 3 tablespoons sugar
- 2 tablespoons khus khus (poppy seeds)
- 2 tablespoons ginger-green chilli paste
- 4 tablespoons lemon juice
- 1 cup chopped coriander leaves
- Salt to taste

For the covering
- 2 1/4 cups gram flour
- 1 teaspoon asafoetida
- 1/2 teaspoon turmeric powder
- 1/2 cup oil
- Oil for frying
- Salt to taste

Method

1 Roast all the ingredients for the masala paste using 1 teaspoon oil. Cool and make into a powder; then add a little water to make the masala paste.

2 Mix all the ingredients for the filling together.
3 Prepare a dough by mixing together all the ingredients for the covering; knead well and divide into 6 balls.
4 Roll out each ball into a big circle. First apply masala paste evenly; then spread the filling. Carefully make a roll. Press well so that the filling does not come out. Cut into 1″ thick pieces.
5 Deep fry in oil over medium heat. Fry to get a golden brown colour. Cool and store.

METHI SHAKKARPARA (CRISPY FENUGREEK SNACK)

PREPARATION TIME: 10 MINS. • COOKING TIME: 30 MINS.

MAKES MANY PIECES

Ingredients

1 cup wheat flour
1 cup flour
1/4 cup gram flour
2 cups chopped fenugreek leaves (methi)
4 tablespoons oil
1/2 teaspoon turmeric powder
2 teaspoons red chilli powder
1 tablespoon ginger-green chilli paste
1/4 teaspoon asafoetida
Oil for frying
Salt to taste

Method

1 Place the fenugreek leaves on a thali and add the salt and sugar and rub the leaves till soft and watery. Now add the flour, wheat flour, gram flour, all the spices and oil; mix thoroughly. Add extra water to make a puri-like dough. Knead well, make large balls and roll out into big circles. Use a little dry flour while rolling. Cut into diamond shaped pieces.
2 Heat the oil and deep fry the shakkarpara till they turn crisp and a light golden colour. Remove onto a piece of absorbent paper to remove the excess oil. They can be stored for a few days and will remain crisp.

KALMI BADE

PREPARATION TIME: 6 HOURS 15 MINS.
COOKING TIME: 45 MINS.
MAKES ABOUT 40 BADE

Ingredients

For the Kalmi Bade

2 cups chana dal (Bengal gram, split)
1/4 teaspoon asafoetida
2 tablespoons coriander seeds
1 tablespoon sesame seeds
3/4 teaspoon coarse black pepper powder
Salt to taste

For the Red Chutney

10 dry red chillies
2 teaspoons amchoor (dry mango powder)
A big pinch of asafoetida
Salt to taste

Method

1 Soak the chana dal for 6 hours. Add the asafoetida and grind with a minimum of water. Add the rest of the seasonings and mix well. Fry large-sized Bade (3″ × 3″ square and 3/4″ thick). Only half cook until they are a light brown; cool and cut into 1/2″ thick pieces.

2 Before serving, refry the Kalmi Bade to get a crisp golden colour. Serve hot with Red Chutney.

3 For the chutney, soak the red chillies in water for 2 hours. Add the other ingredients and blend to make the chutney.

PALAK KE ROLLS (SPINACH NUTTY ROLLS)

PREPARATION TIME: 20 MINS. • COOKING TIME: 35 MINS.
MAKES 20 ROLLS

Ingredients

3 cups boiled and mashed potatoes,
1/2 cup spinach and 4 green chillies, made into a thick paste
2 tablespoons lemon juice
2 tablespoons corn flour
1 tablespoon oil
1 cup peanuts, roasted and coarsely ground
Oil for deep frying
Salt to taste

Method

1 Heat the oil and add the spinach-chilli paste, potatoes, salt, lemon juice and corn flour. Mix well until the mixture turns dry. Remove and cool.

2 Divide the mixture into 20 parts and make long rolls. Cover the rolls by dipping them in ground peanuts. Deep fry in oil till crisp. Serve hot with tomato ketchup.

DAHIWALE SAMOSE
(CURD SAMOSAS)

PREPARATION TIME: 30 MINS. • COOKING TIME: 30 MINS.

MAKES 24 SAMOSAS

Ingredients

For the filling

2 1/2 cups curd
1/2 cup grated cucumber
1 teaspoon cummin seeds, roasted and powdered
2 teaspoons red chilli powder
Salt to taste

For the covering

1 1/2 cups flour
2 tablespoons ghee
1/4 teaspoon salt
Oil for deep frying

Method

1 Place the curd on a fine sieve and drain off water completely.
2. Squeeze out water completely from the grated cucumber and add it to the curd; mix in all the other spices. Put the curd in the refrigerator.
3 Make a dough with the flour, ghee and salt, kneading well and divide into 12 balls. Roll each ball into a 5″ diameter and cut into two. Fold each half into a cone; put in the curd-cucumber filling and seal the edges with a little water to make the samosas.
4. Deep fry in oil until golden brown. Serve hot with tomato ketchup or Green Coriander Chutney (refer to chapter on Pickles, Chutnies & Masalas)

PAV VADA
(POTATO VADA IN BUNS)

PREPARATION TIME: 30 MINS. • COOKING TIME: 20 MINS.

MAKES 6 VADE

Ingredients

6 pav (small square buns)
Butter as required
Oil for deep frying
1/2 cup gram flour
A pinch of soda bicarbonate
Salt to taste

For the vadas

1 1/2 cups boiled and mashed potatoes
3 green chillies
6 cloves garlic, minced
2 tablespoons oil
1/2 teaspoon mustard seeds
1/2 teaspoon turmeric powder

For the red hot chutney

2 teaspoons red chilli powder
1/2 teaspoon cummin seeds, roasted and powdered
10 cloves garlic, optional
A big pinch of black pepper powder

A few curry leaves
Salt to taste

For the covering
$^1/_2$ cup wheat flour
1 teaspoon amchoor (dry mango powder)
A pinch of asafoetida
Salt to taste

Method

1 Heat the oil and add the mustard seeds. When they stop sputtering, add the green chillies, garlic and curry leaves and stir. After a minute, add in the potatoes, turmeric powder and salt. Mix well and remove from the stove. Cool and make 6 balls.
2 To prepare the covering, mix all the ingredients mentioned, with water, to make a thin batter. Dip each potato ball into the batter and deep fry in oil until golden brown.
3 To make the chutney, take all the ingredients in a mixer, add a little water and blend to get a spreading consistency.
4 Split open the pavs, first apply the butter and then the red hot chutney. Put a vada into each and serve.

FRANKIE

PREPARATION TIME: 20 MINS. • COOKING TIME: 45 MINS.
MAKES 6 FRANKIES

Ingredients

For the stuffing
$1^1/_2$ cups boiled and mashed potatoes
2 teaspoons oil
1 teaspoon red chilli powder
2 teaspoons corn flour
1 teaspoon cummin seeds
Salt to taste

For the covering
1 cup flour
2 teaspoons oil
Oil for shallow frying
Salt to taste

For the topping
$^1/_4$ cup white vinegar
2 green chillies, finely chopped
1 onion, finely chopped
Salt and pepper to taste

Method

1 Heat the oil and brown the cummin seeds. Add the potatoes, red chilli powder, salt and corn flour. Mix well and remove from the stove. Cool and divide into 6 portions. Make long rolls of about 4 inches. Roll in corn flour and deep fry in oil till they turn a light brown colour.

2 For the covering take the flour, salt and oil in a vessel. Add water and mix well to make a pancake batter. Set aside for 15 minutes. Then make 6 thin pancakes of 6″ diameter each.
3 To prepare the topping, soak the green chillies in vinegar for at least 1 hour.
4 To assemble a frankie, take 1 pancake, sprinkle the finely chopped onions, salt, pepper, a few green chillies and vinegar. Put a potato roll in the centre. First fold the lower half over the potato roll and then fold sides to enclose the roll tightly inside. Wrap in a paper napkin and serve hot.
5. Make all the frankies in the same way.

CHATPATI SEV
(CRISP SPICY FRIED SNACK)

PREPARATION TIME: 30 MINS. • COOKING TIME: 30 MINS.
SERVES 6-8

Ingredients

1 cucumber, finely chopped
1 tomato, finely chopped
1 onion, finely chopped
Green Coriander chutney
Sweet and Sour Chutney made from dates
Chaat masala
Salt and red chilli powder to taste

For the rice sev

1 1/4 cups rice flour
1 3/4 cups water
1/4 teaspoon black pepper powder
1/4 teaspoon soda bicarbonate
Salt to taste

For the potato sev

2 potatoes, boiled and mashed
1/2 teaspoon ginger-green chilli paste
1 tablespoon lemon juice
2-3 drops yellow colouring
Salt to taste

Chatpati Sev –

For the Green Coriander and Sweet and Sour Chutnies, refer to the chapter on Pickles, Chutnies & Masalas.

Method

For the rice sev

1 Boil water with salt, pepper and soda bicarbonate. Add the rice flour and stir with a wooden spoon, mixing thoroughly to avoid lumps. Cook until the mixture leaves the sides of the vessel. Remove from the stove, cover and set aside for a few minutes.

2 When it cools put the mixture in a sev-making machine; press and drop sev (size of spaghetti) onto a steel plate or dish with holes. Steam again for a few minutes. Invert onto a serving plate.

For the potato sev

1 Mix all the ingredients thoroughly; press and drop through a sev machine onto the previously made rice sev.

To serve

1 Put the rice sev on a serving plate. Sprinkle the salt, red chilli powder and chaat masala; add the cucumber, tomato and onion pieces and pour both the chutnies onto it.

2 Garnish with potato sev and coriander leaves on top.

SEVAI KE CHILKE (VERMICELLI PANCAKES)

PREPARATION TIME: 5-7 MINS. • COOKING TIME: 1 HOUR 40 MINS.

MAKES 10 PANCAKES

Ingredients

1 cup vermicelli, crushed
1 cup semolina
4 green chillies, chopped
1 cup curd
1/4 cup chopped coriander leaves
1/4 cup grated coconut
3 tablespoons ghee
1/4 teaspoon soda bicarbonate
Oil for shallow frying
Salt to taste

Method

1 Melt the ghee and add the green chillies. After a minute, add the vermicelli and semolina. Roast on low heat till it turns light pink in colour. Remove from heat and cool.

2 Add the curd, coriander leaves, coconut, soda bicarbonate and salt to the vermicelli and semolina mixture. Then add enough water to make a pancake batter. Cover and soak for 1 hour.

3 Make golden pancakes on a non-stick griddle with a little oil. Serve hot with Green Coriander Chutney (refer to chapter on Pickles, Chutnies & Masalas).

SWEETS

No meal is complete without a helping of sweets. In some parts of India, sweets are often served along with the main dishes in a traditional *thali*, but for a buffet style meal, they are served as desserts at the end. Some traditional recipes are rich and take time to prepare, such as all varieties of ladoos which are made and served for festivals. Some sweets are light and quick to make, such as halwas, and these are served on all occasions. Try your hand at making and enjoying these wonderful recipes.

(a decorative metal box used for carrying sweets)

1 **Safed Ladoo** p. 89
2 **Churma Ladoo** p. 84
3 **Besan Ke Ladoo** p. 84

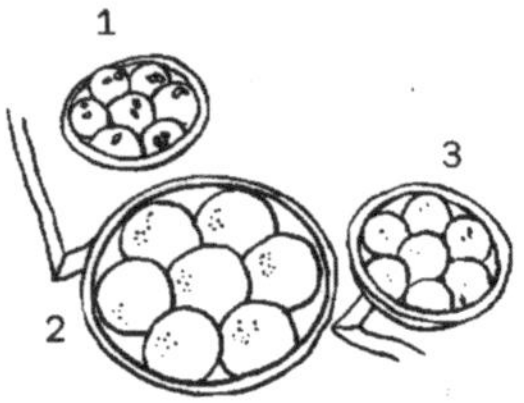

Colour photo on p. 85

---

1 **Chikoo Ke Minar** p. 90
2 **Anjir Ke Chowkan** p. 90

Colour photo on p. 86

BESAN KE LADOO
(SWEET GRAM FLOUR BALLS)

PREPARATION TIME: 1 HOUR 10 MINS.
COOKING TIME: 40 MINS.
MAKES 15 LADOOS

Ingredients

2 cups coarse gram flour
1/3 cup milk
1 tablespoon ghee (for the milk)
1 1/4 cups ghee
1 cup powdered sugar
1 teaspoon cardamom powder
1/4 cup sliced almonds

Method

1 Add the melted ghee and the milk to the gram flour and mix well. Cover and set aside for 1/2 hour. Strain through a coarse sieve to make it grainy.
2 Melt the rest of the ghee in a thick-bottomed vessel. Add the prepared flour and roast till it turns light pink. Now add the powdered sugar, cardamom and sliced almonds. Remove from the stove and cool. While the mixture is still warm, make small, round, ball-shaped ladoos.

CHURMA LADOO
(SWEET WHEAT FLOUR BALLS)

PREPARATION TIME: 15 MINS. • COOKING TIME: 50 MINS.
MAKES 12 LADOOS

Ingredients

2 cups wheat flour (preferably coarse)
3/4 cup ghee
1 1/4 cups jaggery
1/2 cup dry grated coconut
2 tablespoons khus khus (poppy seeds)
Ghee for frying

Method

1 In a thali, take the wheat flour and melted ghee. Mix thoroughly to make a stiff dough with water or milk. Make balls in the shape of a fist with depression of fingers.
2 Heat the ghee and deep fry the balls on a low flame till golden brown. Remove and cool. Break up the balls using your fingers and crush them or put into a mixer and grind into a very coarse powder. Strain through a coarse sieve.
3 In a vessel, melt the jaggery on a low flame and stir till it starts bubbling. Add the grated coconut and mix well. Pour this over the wheat mixture, mixing thoroughly. Make the ladoos while the mixture is still warm. Roll each ladoo in poppy seeds and arrange on a plate for serving.

SUJI GHUGHARA
(CRIPSY FRIED SEMOLINA SWEET)

PREPARATION TIME: 15 MINS. • COOKING TIME: 1 HOUR
MAKES 25 GHUGHARAS

Ingredients

For the filling

1½ cups suji (semolina)
½ cup melted ghee
¼ cup dry grated coconut
½ teaspoon cardamom powder
¾ cup powdered sugar

For the covering

2 cups flour
¼ cup melted ghee
25 cloves
Ghee for deep frying

Method

1 Melt the ghee and roast the suji in it over a slow fire till it turns a light pink colour. Add the coconut and cardamom powder. Mix well and remove from the stove. Cool and mix in the powdered sugar.
2 Make a puri-like dough with the flour and ghee kneading well. Divide into 25 pieces and keep covered.
3 Roll out each portion into a puri; put in the filling and close to form a half circle. Press the edges firmly. Decorate edges by the pinch and press method. Push a clove through the centre. Deep fry in ghee till they turn a light pink colour.

SAFED LADOO
(SWEET WHITE BALLS)

PREPARATION TIME: 10 MINS. • COOKING TIME: 30 MINS.
MAKES 15 LADOOS

Ingredients

1½ cups suji (semolina)
2 cups khoya (mawa)
½ cup chopped almonds and pistachios
2 teaspoons cardamom powder
1½ cups sugar
¾ cup ghee
A few drops lemon juice

Method

1 Break up the khoya by passing it through a large-holed sieve.
2 Heat the ghee and roast the semolina over a low flame till the semolina turns light pink. Add the khoya and roast for another 2-3 minutes. Remove from the stove and cool.
3 Take the sugar in a vessel and add just enough water to dissolve it. Add a few drops of lemon juice to remove any dirt; strain. Return the vessel to the stove and cook till the sugar syrup forms a two-thread consistency (thick syrup). Cool and mix with the semolina, khoya, cardamom powder and nuts. Mix well and then make small ladoos.

Suji Ghughara –
To decorate the edge of the ghughara, press the dough between the tips of the thumb and the first finger. Turn it and fold inward. Then press again, forming a continuous design.

1 **Chhunda** p. 98
2 **Nimbu Ka Achar** p. 100
3 **Mirchi Ka Achar** p. 98
4 **Lal Mirchi Ka Achar** p. 99

Colour photo on p. 88

1 **Shahi Malai Tukade** p. 91
2 **Paneer Ki Kheer** p. 93

Colour photo on p. 87

CHICKOO KE MINAR
(CHIKOO TOWERS)

PREPARATION TIME: 10 MINS. • COOKING TIME: 30 MINS.
MAKES 10 TOWERS

Ingredients

2 cups chikoo pulp
1 $^1/_2$ cups sugar
1 cup khoya (mawa)
$^1/_4$ cup cashewnuts, small pieces.
20 cashewnuts, halved
$^1/_2$ teaspoon cardamom powder

Method

1 Combine the chikoo pulp and sugar in a non-stick pan. Stir continuously with a wooden spoon over a low flame till the sugar melts and the mixture becomes thick. Add the mawa and small cashewnut pieces. Mix well and simmer till the mixture leaves the sides of the vessel. Add the cardamom powder and mix well. Cool a little. Make tall rounds (towers) and decorate with halved cashewnut pieces.

ANJIR KE CHOWKAN
(FIG SQUARES)

PREPARATION TIME: 10 MINS. • COOKING TIME: 30 MINS.
MAKES 20 PIECES

Ingredients

$^1/_4$ kg. dry figs (anjeer), chopped
1 litre milk
$^1/_2$ cup dry grated coconut
$^1/_2$ teaspoon cardamom powder
$^1/_2$ cup sugar
A few slices almonds and pistachios

Method

1 Wash, clean, and chop the figs. Add the milk and cook. When the milk is thicker and the quantity less, crush the figs into a pulp, although a few large pieces may remain. Add the sugar and dry coconut.

2. Put back on the stove and cook till the mixture leaves the sides of the vessel. Remove onto a thali and set. Sprinkle almonds and pistachios slices. Cut into square pieces and serve.

SHAHI MALAI TUKADE
(CREAMY ROYAL SWEET)

PREPARATION TIME: 10 MINS. • COOKING TIME: 1 HOUR

MAKES 10 PIECES

Ingredients

10 slices of bread
1 litre milk
1/3 cup sugar
1/4 teaspoon cardamom powder
150 gms. khoya (mawa)
3 tablespoons powdered sugar (for the khoya)
1/2 cup home-made paneer
2 tablespoons icing sugar (for the paneer)
A pinch of saffron
Ghee for deep frying
A few slices of almonds and pistachios

Method

1 Cut the slices of bread into round circles. Deep fry in ghee till golden brown.

2 Warm the milk with the sugar and cardamom powder.

3 Put 2 of the fried bread circles into a shallow non-stick frying pan. Pour milk to cover them and simmer on the stove till the milk is absorbed; turn sides. When properly soaked but dry, gently remove the bread slices onto a plate. Do the same with all the circles.

4 Combine the khoya, dissolved saffron and powdered sugar on a plate till you get a spreading consistency. Spread some on each side.

5 Mix the paneer and icing sugar thoroughly in a bowl or in a mixer, to make a smooth paste. Obtain a piping consistency. You may have to add a little milk. Fill the prepared paneer into a piping bag fitted with a star nozzle. Decorate each Shahi Tukada with almond and pistachios slices and some paneer.

Bundi Halwa –

To dissolve saffron, warm it in a small steel vessel till crisp. Crush and add a spoonful of milk. Mix thoroughly.

BHUTTE KE GOLE
(CORN PUFFS)

PREPARATION TIME: 20 MINS. • COOKING TIME: 45 MINS.

MAKES 20 PUFFS

Ingredients

For the filling

1 cup fresh corn, grated
2 tablespoons ghee
1 cup milk
1/2 cup sugar
1/4 teaspoon cardamom powder
A little saffron, dissolved in milk

For the covering

1 cup flour
1/4 cup semolina
4 tablespoons ghee
Khus khus (poppy seeds) for sprinkling
Ghee for deep frying

Method

1 To prepare the filling, heat the ghee and add the corn, stirring continuously till it changes colour. Add the milk and mix well. When the milk has been almost absorbed, add the sugar, cardamom powder and dissolved saffron. Continue cooking till the mixture thickens and leaves the sides of the vessel. Remove from the stove and cool. Make 20 small balls.

2 To prepare the dough, mix the flour, semolina and ghee. Make a puri-like dough and knead it well. Divide into 20 balls.

3 Now flatten each ball and stuff with some corn filling; roll gently. Deep fry in ghee to get a light pink colour and make it crisp.

4. Sprinkle a few grains of khus khus on each puff.

BUNDI HALWA

PREPARATION TIME: 5 MINS. • COOKING TIME: 35 MINS.

SERVES 6

Ingredients

2 cups plain saltless bundi (readymade)
2 cups milk
1 cup khoya (mawa)
1 1/4 cups sugar
A little saffron, dissolved
A few pistachio slices

Method

1 Soak the bundi in milk for 15 minutes. Add the sugar and boil; simmer till it starts thickening. Mix the mawa and saffron. Simmer till the bundi halwa leaves the sides of the vessel. Remove onto a thali and set.

2 Decorate with pistachio slices.

PANEER KI KHEER (COTTAGE CHEESE IN THICKENED MILK)

PREPARATION TIME: 5 MINS. • COOKING TIME: 45 MINS.

SERVES 6

Ingredients

1 litre milk
3/4 cup sugar
1/2 cup cooking paneer, cut into very small cubes
1 teaspoon lemon juice
2 tablespoons chopped almonds and pistachios
1/4 teaspoon cardamom, powdered

Method

1 Take 1/4 of the milk in an iron vessel (kadai) and simmer for rapid thickening. Dissolve the sugar in the heated milk. Add 3-4 drops of lemon juice and continue simmering till the milk reduces to half its original quantity. Empty the thickened milk into another vessel. Repeat the boiling process each time with 1/4 litre of milk.

2 Add the paneer cubes and cardamom powder to the hot, thickened milk (kheer). Mix thoroughly and cool. Sprinkle almonds and pistachios before serving in a bowl.

SHRIKHAND

PREPARATION TIME: 3 HOURS • NO COOKING

SERVES 3

Ingredients

1 cup powdered sugar or sugar to taste
4 cups thick curd

Method

1 Place the curd on a fine sieve and drain off its whey. The curd will reduce to nearly 2 cups.

2 Add in the powdered sugar and mix well in a blender. Strain again to make a very smooth thick paste.

3 Chill in the refrigerator till you wish to serve.

This is the basic Shrikhand mixture. There are many ways to flavour it. Here are two ways :

(A) Kesari Shrikhand
Mix in 1/2 teaspoon cardamom powder and 1/4 teaspoon saffron (dissolved in a little milk), to the Shrikhand. Sprinkle almond and pistachio slices.

(B) Fruit Shrikhand
Pieces of any of the following fruits – strawberry, mango, pineapple, grapes, chikoo or a mixture of fruits – can be added to the Shrikhand.

Paneer Ki Kheer –

(a) To make paneer cubes, wrap the paneer in a muslin cloth and press thoroughly by applying a heavy weight on it for 30 minutes. Then cut into small cubes.

(b) An iron kadai is like a Chinese wok.

SITAFAL KI MITHAI (CUSTARD APPLE SURPRISE)

PREPARATION TIME: 10 MINS. • COOKING TIME: 45 MINS.

MAKES 15 PIECES

Ingredients

For the filling

1/2 cup pulp of custard apple
3/4 cup khoya (mawa)
3 tablespoons sugar
1/4 teaspoon vanilla essence

For the covering

1 cup thin flattened rice (nylon poha)
3/4 cup sugar
1 1/2 tablespoons ghee
2 cups milk
1/2 cup khoya
A few strands saffron, crushed
Silver foil (varakh) for decorating

Method

For the filling

1 Mix all the ingredients together and put on the stove. Stir constantly till it thickens and leaves the sides of the vessel. Cool.

For the covering

1 Clean and wash the poha and mash. Melt the ghee in a vessel; add the poha and stir for a few minutes. Then add in the milk, sugar and khoya and simmer till it becomes very thick and leaves the sides of the vessel. Add the crushed saffron, mix well and remove from the stove. Cool and divide into 15 balls.

2 Flatten each portion of covering, place filling in the centre and roll into a round ball. Decorate with silver foil on top. You can put each ball into a small butter-paper cup.

SUKHE MEWE KI BARFI
(DRY FRUIT BARFIS)

PREPARATION TIME: 30 MINS. • COOKING TIME: 40 MINS.

MAKES 20 BARFIS

Ingredients

200 gms. dry figs (anjeer)
3/4 cup milk
3/4 cup sugar
300 gms. khoya (mawa)
1/4 cup powdered cashewnuts
1 1/2 tablespoons ghee
1/4 cup chopped almonds and pistachios
1/4 teaspoon cardamom powder
Silver varakh
Paper cups

Method

1 Chop the figs into small pieces and soak in milk for 1/2 hour.
2 In a thick-bottomed vessel, heat ghee and sauté the fig pieces for 2-3 minutes; add the sugar and cook till the milk evaporates.
3 Add the mawa and cook for another 5-7 minutes. Add the powdered cashewnuts, almonds, pistachios and cardamom powder. Mix well and remove from the stove to cool.
4 While the mixture is still warm, form into balls and arrange them in paper cups. Decorate with silver varakh.

KESAR MALAI PEDA
(CREAMY SAFFRON PEDAS)

PREPARATION TIME: 5 MINS. • COOKING TIME: 50 MINS.

MAKES 24 PEDAS

Ingredients

1 litre milk
150 gms. sugar
1/4 teaspoon citric acid
1 teaspoon corn flour, dissolved in cold water
1/4 teaspoon saffron, dissolved in a little milk
1/4 teaspoon cardamom powder
A few pistachios for decoration

Method

1 Boil the milk in a thick-bottomed vessel till it reduces to half the original quantity. Add the sugar and boil for another 5-7 minutes, stirring continuously.
2 Dissolve the citric acid in a teaspoon of water; add it gradually to the boiling milk, stirring constantly till the milk is almost dry. Add the saffron and cardamom powder.
3 The mixture should collect like a soft ball. Remove from the stove and cool. Make into slightly flattened balls while the mixture is still warm. Decorate with sliced pistachios.

Sukhe Mewe Ki Barfi –

(a) Silver varakh is beaten silver which is, used to decorate Indian sweets.

(b) Khoya is readily available in India and is also called mawa. To make it, boil milk in a thick-bottomed broad vessel, stirring often until a thick residue remains. Using a non-stick pan is ideal. Squeezing a few drops of lemon juice in the boiling milk hastens the process.

Shahi Aam Firni–

Firni can be put into earthenware bowls and set separately for individual servings.

SHAHI AAM FIRNI (ROYAL MANGO PUDDING)

PREPARATION TIME: 10 MINS. • COOKING TIME: 40 MINS.
SERVES 6-8

Ingredients

1 cup vermicelli, crushed
1 litre milk
3/4 cup sugar
3/4 cup mango pulp (fresh or canned)
2 tablespoons ghee
200 gms. fresh cream
3 teaspoons gelatin
4 tablespoons powdered sugar
A few almonds, blanched and sliced
A few mango pieces, to decorate

Method

1. Sauté the vermicelli in ghee till it is a light pink. Add the milk and boil for a few minutes. Add the sugar and continue to simmer till 1/2 of the milk evaporates. Remove from the stove and cool to room temperature.
2. Dissolve gelatin in a little hot water. Add this to the milk and vermicelli mixture. Refrigerate to chill.
3. Beat the fresh cream with the powdered sugar till it is thicker but still flowing. Mix 1/2 of it into the semi-set mixture. Also mix in the mango pulp. Pour into a serving bowl and set it in the refrigerator.
4. Beat the remaining fresh cream till stiff. Decorate the firni with sliced almonds, mango pieces and cream. Serve chilled.

CHOCOLATE HALWA

PREPARATION TIME: 7 MINS. • COOKING TIME: 30 MINS.
MAKES 12 PIECES

Ingredients

10 slices of bread
1 cup khoya (mawa)
1 cup milk
1 cup sugar
2 tablespoons cocoa powder
1/2 teaspoon vanilla essence
1/4 cup cashewnut pieces
Silver varakh

Method

1. Remove the crusts from the slices of bread and break the bread into small pieces.
2. Dissolve the sugar and cocoa powder in the milk (warm milk if necessary). Soak the bread pieces in the milk for 10 minutes and mash to a pulp. Cook till the milk is absorbed.
3. Mix the khoya, cashewnut pieces and vanilla essence thoroughly and cook till the halwa leaves the sides of the vessel. Spread out evenly on a serving plate. Decorate with silver foil and cut into small pieces before serving.

Pickles Chutnies & Masalas

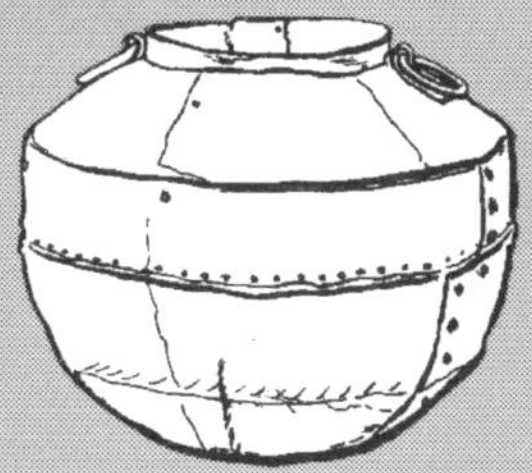

(a large storage jar for edible oils)

As summer arrives, one starts looking out for good quality spices to be stored for the year. There are many varieties of dry chillies available on the market. Some are shiny, bright red and mild, while others are small, dark red and very hot. Select the type that you and your family would prefer. Some of the basic combinations of spices are called *masalas*. They useful in the preparation of Indian vegetarian dishes.

Pickles can be made from many different fruits and vegetables, such as lemons or chillies but raw mango makes the queen of pickles; moreover, hot mango pickle is the king of all pickles. There is a saying that pickles and chutnies can save money and many an occasion. Serving pickles with meals is usual during summer time in rural India, as fresh vegetable produce and its supply declines and consequently they become expensive. At such times, pickles come in handy. Apart from imparting a tickling taste, the hot chillies and salt in the pickles also help in opening up perspiration glands and maintaining the body salt level.

No *thali* looks complete without at least one pickle and a chutney. You can make many varieties of freshly ground chutnies to accompany savouries and Indian breads like puris and parathas.

CHHUNDA
(SWEET AND SOUR MANGO PICKLE)

Ingredients

6 raw mangoes – (Rajapuri variety if possible) peeled and grated to measure 10 cups
15 cups sugar
3/4 cup salt
1/2 cup cummin seeds, roasted and coarsely powdered
1 cup red chilli powder

Method

1 Mix the grated raw mango and salt. Keep mixing till a good amount of water oozes out.

2 Add the sugar and mix well till the sugar almost disappears. Cover and set aside for 12-24 hours.

3 Tie a thin cloth over the mouth of the Chhunda vessel. Place this vessel in the scorching sun. Stir the Chhunda every evening. Place the vessel in a thali full of water to avoid crawling insects getting into the vessel. Continue this process every day till the sugar syrup gets fairly thick or when a drop of syrup put on a plate does not run but remains steady in one place.

4 Now mix in the cummin seeds powder and red chilli powder and leave the Chhunda in the sun for 1 more day. Next day, fill the Chhunda in a glass jar. This can be preserved for more than a year.

Precaution : Sun-scorching is best carried out during the hottest summer months.

MIRCHI KA ACHAR
(CHILLI PICKLE)

Ingredients

1/2 kg. good quality long green chillies, cut into pieces
1/2 cup salt
1 tablespoon turmeric powder
1 teaspoon asafoetida
1/2 cup mustard seeds powder
4 tablespoons lemon juice
2 tablespoons oil

Method

1 Prepare a mixture of salt, turmeric powder, mustard powder and asafoetida. Rub this on the chilli pieces. Fill in a bottle with the chillies. Add the lemon juice and mix well.

2 Set aside for a day and the next day put in the oil. Mix well and use after 2-3 days. This pickle can be preserved in the refrigerator for 2-3 weeks.

LAL MIRCHI KA ACHAR
(RED CHILLI PICKLE)

Ingredients

500 gms. fresh red chillies
Oil as required

For the stuffing

150 gms. amchoor (dry mango powder)
2 tablespoons salt
50 gms. mustard kuria (coarse powder)
2 tablespoons kalonji (onion seeds)
50 gms. fenugreek kuria (coarse powder)
1 tablespoon cummin seeds, roasted and powdered
½ teaspoon asafoetida
½ cup ani seeds (saunf)

Method

1 Remove the stems and seeds from the chillies. You may retain a few seeds to make the pickle hot. Mix all the ingredients for the stuffing except the oil. Fill the chillies tightly with the masala stuffing.

2 In a vessel, arrange the chillies in an upright position, standing side by side. Pour enough oil to soak the masala in each chilli. Keep for a few days, then transfer into a jar. Use after 15 days. This pickle can be preserved for a year.

TIKHA AAM KA ACHAR
(HOT MANGO PICKLE)

Ingredients

25 good quality raw mangoes, cut into square pieces
2 tablespoons turmeric powder
5 cups Hot Pickle Sambhar (page 97)
2 cups sesame (til) oil
4 cups salt

Method

1 Mix 2 cups salt and the turmeric powder with the mango pieces. Cover and set aside for 24 hours; shake a few times. Next day, take out the mango pieces, remove the water and dry them on a cloth, in the shade, for at least 6-8 hours.

2 Then mix in the Sambhar masala and 2 cups of salt and put the pickle into a bottle. Press down the mango pieces and then pour the oil over them. Next day, check the pickle; if the oil has settled, add some more oil. Oil should float on top all the time to avoid fungus. Use the pickle after a few days. This mango pickle can be preserved for a year.

TIKHA ACHAR KA SAMBHAR
(SPICY PICKLE POWDER)

Ingredients

1 cup mustard kuria (coarse powder)
2 cups fenugreek (methi) kuria (a coarse powder)
4 cups red chilli powder
2 tablespoons asafoetida (hing)
2 tablespoons turmeric powder
2 cups oil, preferably sesame oil
5 cups salt

Method

1 Put the asafoetida in the centre of a thali, surround it with a circle of mustard kuria and then fenugreek kuria.
2 Heat the oil and pour it over all 3 things. Cover and allow it to cool.
3 Add the chilli powder and turmeric powder and mix thoroughly. This mixture is the basic raw material for many pickles. It can be stored in a bottle for the whole year and is called Sambhar. Mix salt as and when needed.

NIMBU KA ACHAR
(LEMON PICKLE)

Ingredients

25 good quality lemons, to be washed and dried on a cloth
1 tablespoon turmeric powder
5 tablespoons Hot Pickle Sambhar
2 teaspoons asafoetida
2 tablespoons red chilli powder
Oil as required
$^3/_4$ kg. salt

Method

1 Cut the lemons and split them into 4 for stuffing. Mix the salt and turmeric powder together and stuff each lemon with it very well.
2 In a bottle, place some salt mixture at the bottom; then put in some of the stuffed lemons and a layer of salt mixture at the top. Cover. Shake every day and check occasionally. After about $1^1/_2$ months, the lemons will be ready for pickling.
3 Cut each lemon into small pieces. Mix the asafoetida, sambhar and chilli powder. Add a little oil if you like. Mix well and add to the lemons in the bottle.

KHATTI–MITHI CHUTNEY (SWEET & SOUR CHUTNEY)

Ingredients

$^{1}/_{2}$ kg. dates
150 gms. tamarind
100 gms. jaggery
1 teaspoon cummin seeds, roasted and powdered
$^{1}/_{2}$ teaspoon black pepper powder
2 teaspoons red chilli powder
Salt to taste

Method

1 Remove the seeds from the dates and tamarind. Wash and place them in a vessel. Add enough water to cover.
2 Add the jaggery and all the other spices.
3 Pressure cook; cool and blend and then strain to a thick paste. Adjust consistency with water and use as required.

HARI DHANIA KI CHUTNEY (GREEN CORIANDER CHUTNEY)

Ingredients

$^{3}/_{4}$ cup chopped coriander leaves
2 cloves garlic (optional)
2 green chillies
1 tablespoon lemon juice
1 tablespoon dalia (roasted gram, split)
1 tablespoon fresh coconut
Salt to taste

Method

1 First grind the dalia.
2 Then add the coconut, garlic and chillies and grind.
3 Finally, add the coriander, lemon juice and salt and grind again to make a fine paste.

ADARAKH - HARE MIRCHI KI PASTE (GINGER-GREEN CHILLI PASTE)

Ingredients

100 gms. green chillies
$1^{1}/_{2}$ inch ginger
$^{1}/_{2}$ teaspoon salt
1 teaspoon lemon juice

Method

1 Grind all the ingredients in a blender to make a fine paste.

Khatti-Mithi Chutney–

This chutney can be preserved in the refrigerator for a week and up to 3 months in the freezer.

Hari Dhania Ki Chutney–

To make Hari Pudina Ki Chutney, add 10 mint leaves and omit the garlic from the recipe.

HARE TAMATAR KI CHUTNEY
(GREEN TOMATO CHUTNEY)

Ingredients

150 gms. raw green tomatoes
6-10 green chillies
1/2" piece of ginger
1 1/2 teaspoons cummin seeds, roasted and powdered
1/4 teaspoon asafoetida
1/4 cup coriander leaves
1/4 cup grated coconut
2 tablespoons jaggery – optional
Salt to taste

Method

1 Push a fork through a tomato and roast it over a flame till the skin splits. Peel and chop.

2 Roast the green chillies on a griddle. Mix the rest of the ingredients and grind together to make the chutney.

KACHE AAM KA ACHAR
(RAW MANGO PICKLE)

Ingredients

1 cup grated raw mango
1 cup grated onion
1 teaspoon ground cummin seeds, roasted
1/4 cup jaggery
3-5 teaspoons red chilli powder
A pinch of asafoetida
1 teaspoon salt

Method

1 Mix the salt with the grated mangoes and onions. Set aside for 10 minutes. Lightly squeeze out the water. Mix in the rest of the ingredients and fill a jar with it. This fresh pickle can be used for at least a week.

GARAM MASALA
(SPICY POWDER)

MAKES 1/3 CUPS

Ingredients

- 2 tablespoons black peppercorns
- 25 cardamoms
- 25 cinnamon, large pieces
- 100 cloves

Method

Pick and clean all the ingredients. Dry grind till very fine and store in an air-tight bottle.

HARI MIRCH KA ACHAR
(GREEN CHILLI PICKLE)

Ingredients

- 15 green chillies, chopped
- 2 teaspoons aniseed
- 3/4 teaspoon fenugreek
- 1 1/2 teaspoons mustard seeds
- 2 teaspoons amchoor (dry mango powder)
- 2 tablespoons oil
- A big pinch of asafoetida
- 1/2 teaspoon salt

Method

1 Roast the aniseed, fenugreek and mustard seeds till they turn light brown. Mix all the other spices and the oil with the chopped green chillies.

2 Fill a glass jar with the pickle and place in the sun for at least 1/2 hour.

Hari Mirch Ka Achar – This pickle can also be made with raw green mango pieces.

1 Kale Kishmis Ki Chutney p. 104
2 Hari Mirch Ka Achar p. 103
3 Kache Aam Ka Achar p. 102
4 Hare Tamatar Ki Chutney p. 102

Colour photo a p. 105

Black cover :
1 Vitamin Salad
2 Pachadi Salad

CHAAT MASALA

Ingredients

- 1/4 teaspoon asafoetida
- 1 teaspoon black pepper
- 1 teaspoon black salt
- 2 teaspoons cummin seeds, ground and roasted
- 1 teaspoon ginger powder
- 3 teaspoons amchoor (dry mango powder)
- 2 teaspoons red chilli powder
- 1 1/2 teaspoons salt

Method

1 Dry grind all the ingredients to a very fine powder and store in an air-tight bottle.

KALE KISHMIS KI CHUTNEY
(BLACK CURRANT CHUTNEY)

Ingredients

- 1 cup black raisins, deseeded
- 2 tablespoons raisins, chopped
- 1 tablespoon red chilli powder
- 1 teaspoon cummin seeds, powdered and roasted
- 10 mint leaves
- 2 tablespoons jaggery
- 3 teaspoons lemon juice
- 1 teaspoon salt

Method

1 Wash and soak the black raisins in 1/2 cup of luke warm water for 1 hour.
2 Make the chutney in a mixer using the rest of the ingredients (except the raisins). Add the chopped raisins and set aside for at least 1/2 hour before serving.